John DeWitt

What is Inspiration?

A fresh Study of the Question with new and discriminative Replies

John DeWitt

What is Inspiration?
A fresh Study of the Question with new and discriminative Replies

ISBN/EAN: 9783337183370

Printed in Europe, USA, Canada, Australia, Japan

Cover: Foto ©ninafisch / pixelio.de

More available books at **www.hansebooks.com**

WHAT IS INSPIRATION?

*A FRESH STUDY OF THE QUESTION
WITH NEW AND DISCRIMINATIVE REPLIES*

BY

JOHN DE WITT, D.D., LL.D., Litt. D.

A MEMBER OF THE AMERICAN OLD TESTAMENT REVISION COMPANY, AND FOR MANY YEARS PROFESSOR OF BIBLICAL EXEGESIS IN THE THEOLOGICAL SEMINARY AT NEW BRUNSWICK, N. J. AUTHOR OF "THE PSALMS; A NEW TRANSLATION WITH NOTES," ETC.

NEW YORK
ANSON D. F. RANDOLPH
& COMPANY
(INCORPORATED)
182 FIFTH AVENUE

PRESS OF
EDWARD O. JENKINS' SON,
NEW YORK.

Dedication.

This volume is inscribed to the memory of one who was here when it was planned and large portions of it were written. It has received precious consecration from her deep interest in its purpose and progress, and her pleasure in anticipating its publication. Yet she could not wait for the end, but is gone to the reward of her faithful, patient, loving, self-sacrificing, and gracious life.

PREFACE.

This essay is a response to an imperative demand. Any questioning that bears upon the inspiration of the Bible is of like interest and vital importance to all Christians.

The arraignment of two theological Professors for heresy on the ground of their opinions upon this subject, has created great anxiety,—yet not so much the fact of their arraignment, as the vindicatory statements in their defence, and the acceptance of these as satisfactory, if only by a large minority. Opposite decisions have been reached in the lower tribunals, and by many upon both sides the outcome is awaited with apprehension. I am neither a partisan nor an opponent of plaintiff or defendants, and only refer to these proceedings as historic facts that involve principles and results of the deepest concern to us all.

Whatever be the issue as respects the individuals impleaded, it has been claimed and is not denied, that Christian scholarship in this specialty is nearly unanimous in discrediting the *verbal* inspiration and inerrancy of the Scriptures. It cannot be doubted that unprofessional intelligence will be greatly influenced by those who have studied the documents as experts, and in whose ability, attachment to the Bible, and unimpeachable Christian excellence it has absolute confidence.

It is not at all strange that many are greatly distressed. They have never before had a doubt that every word of this treasured Book is divine and faultless, and honestly think that the foundations of their faith are destroyed. "What is inspiration," they ask, "that leaves errors behind it?" They demand something positive,—some conception of the grace that has given us the Bible, that shall reassure them against this appalling negation.

In fact, the question is pressed from all sides: "What definition of inspiration will you substitute for that which scholarship has disparaged?" It is vaguely claimed, some will say, by these adepts and their friends, that the Bible, released from the misconceptions that have obscured it, is a grander book than before. But what proof have we of this, and on what intelligible ground can it be claimed that we shall gain more than we lose?

An answer to these appeals must not be refused. For the opinion gains ground and is strongly expressed, that widespread injury will result from these trials and resultant discussions, unless clear, definite, and conclusive statement shall very soon bring relief to those they have disturbed. A prosecutor in the New York case indignantly exclaims: "Is our doctrine to be thrown aside on the demand of a body of critics who have as yet found nothing to put in its place?" *

The same thought is expressed more fully by a writer in a religious journal † in connection with the case of Prof. Smith: "The least that can be demanded is the concession from the Professor and his class of scholars, that this is an unsettled question. The theory is yet in

---

* Dr. Lampe's reply to Dr. Briggs.
† *The Interior*, Chicago.

the raw. The doctrine has not been wrought out so that one holding it can identify the alleged human from the admittedly divine in Scripture. . . . . Has he not run before his tidings were ready? Has he not broken down before he was ready to rebuild? It is undoubtedly true that the question is one of fact, which lies within the field of scientific research; and if it be found to be true, the church will be forced to reconstruct her theory of inspiration."

In a different tone, but assertive of the same necessity, is an article in a leading New York daily journal on the ethics of the Briggs trial. The writer takes a hopeful view of the future. He refers to all that has recently been said and written on the subject—as " embraced in a campaign of education that will in a reasonably short time change the attitude of the whole Christian world toward the Bible," and he expresses his confidence that it will not end in the depreciation of its contents, nor the refusal to regard it as of divine authority. But he speaks emphatically of "the shock which millions of devout people are receiving, as they find that they have put an estimate upon the Bible that is altogether different from what a knowledge of its character and claims will sustain, as greatly to be regretted. . . . . The pressure of the heresy trials in the Presbyterian body has hastened the distress of these people, and done nothing to supply the loss which has been caused by partially destroying their confidence in the Bible."

Nothing can be clearer than the obligation of those who have rejected the theory of verbal inspiration, as not in accordance with what they find by the most careful scrutiny of the contents of the Bible, to furnish with the least possible delay a definition that shall replace it as consistent with undeniable fact, and thus quiet the prevailing agitation.

In preparing the following chapters it was impossible to conceal my deep interest in the recent discussions in their important practical bearings, and so I have occasionally referred to them. I have spent the larger portion of my active life in giving instruction in the Old and New Testaments, separately and in their connection. Every year, and month, and day, they have become more precious, and all labor in developing their glorious import, and their significance in connection with every aspiration and hope of man, has become more absorbing. I have therefore felt conscientiously impelled to render this further service, hoping that the thoughts presented, however doubtful or perplexing to some in their earlier impression, may prove helpful and restful in their conclusions.

I rejoice that I am permitted to magnify the grace that has been shown me, in urging the claim of him who came down from heaven to show us the Father, to pre-eminence over all others as the Teacher of men. The principles that are observed in defining inspiration in the closing chapters, I pass over to younger men to test and develop. If they seek it, their heart and their lips shall be touched with fire from above, and they shall speak as was impossible for me. May the dear Lord help them!

Then shall our present apprehensions be completely quelled, and we shall find a charming significance for our present need in our Saviour's words of farewell: "Peace I leave with you. My peace I give unto you. Not as the world giveth, give I unto you. Let not your heart be troubled, neither let it be afraid."

CONTENTS.

	PAGE
I. Preliminary,	1
II. Verbal or Plenary Inspiration,	9
III. Inspiration and the earlier Biblical Study,	16
IV. Two Theologies in Contrast,	23
V. The Higher Criticism, Destructive and Constructive,	31
VI. Minor Inaccuracies,	37
VII. Minor Inaccuracies—Historical,	45
VIII. Moral Incongruities,	58
IX. Turning Forward — General Considerations,	68
X. Inspiration defined by Revelation,	78
XI. The Human Coefficient in Revelation,	86
XII. Revelation keeping pace with Development,	97
XIII. The Revelation as addressed to Men,	103
XIV. Hope long deferred,	115
XV. Hope long deferred—Continued,	130
XVI. The Purpose of the Revelation,	139
XVII. The Glory of the Old Testament Revelation,	146
XVIII. The Prophets — The Christ — The Apostles,	154
XIX. The Discriminative Definition in part,	161
XX. The Definition Completed and the Final Test,	166
XXI. The Final Test—Continued,	174

WHAT IS INSPIRATION?

I.

PRELIMINARY.

A FEW months ago, at the close of a letter upon personal affairs to a highly gifted friend, a postscript was added containing only this question: "What is inspiration?"

He understood it, as was intended, to relate wholly to the Bible. His reply was as follows,—this also in postscript: "You ask, 'What is inspiration?' Would that the Lord would raise up and inspire some one of his servants to give a reasonably clear answer to your question. I have not found such an one, though I have been looking for him for some time."

We all believe that God often gives such aid, enabling those who receive it to use their faculties to better purpose than would otherwise be possible.

A remarkable story is told in the annals of the Westminster Assembly concerning George Gillespie of Edinburgh, the youngest member of that body. It is the same George Gillespie of whom it is related that he was requested by the Moderator, in view of the difficulty that was found in framing for the Catechism a suitable definition of God, to lead the Assembly in prayer for divine aid, and the first sentence of whose prayer was immediately and unanimously adopted as containing the answer sought. This further instance of a similar kind is on record: A day was appointed by the Assembly for considering the nature and constitution of the Christian Church. Great anxiety was felt by the Presbyterian divines, principally because the leader of the Erastian party, who would have subjected the Church to the State, was John Selden, the most learned man in England. He was especially strong in Rabbinic lore, from which, in connection with the constitution of the Jewish synagogue, his opinions on the subject were derived.

His argument was masterly, and apparently unanswerable. The representatives of Presbyterianism stood aghast and thought their cause lost. But some one who had observed that while Selden was speaking the young Scotchman Gillespie seemed to be diligently taking notes, earnestly beckoned to him to reply. He did so promptly, taking up Selden's argument point by point, and tore it into shreds and tatters, to the entire discomfiture of Erastianism.

After the debate was closed, one that sat near Gillespie managed to get hold of the paper on which he had been writing, expecting to find a full sketch of his effort, or at least, its principal points. But it contained only the simple words, "*Da lucem, Domine! Da lucem, Domine!*" (Give light, O Lord!) written again and again from the top to the bottom of the page.

WHAT IS IT?

There is no subject upon which light from the source of all light is at present more needed than the inspiration of the Scriptures. Let all Christian hearts unite in imploring it.

The most suitable expression of the scope, contents, and spirit of the following pages is interrogative. Is it possible to adjust our theory and definition of the inspiring grace that has given us the Bible to the facts that have been ascertained by its critical and conscientious study during the last half century?

The question relates to the theory of verbal inspiration in both its forms, the mechanical and the plenary, as not in accord with the observed phenomena of revelation. By this test every proposed definition, however plausible and satisfactory *a priori*, must stand or fall. There should be no conflict between our ideal and the actual. Whatever it has pleased God to give us as suited to our need should be gratefully accepted. Our ideal, if different, is a delusion.

Hitherto, by common consent, the subject has been referred to the future. Definition has been held in abeyance, by the wisest and safest men, until the ground should be thoroughly explored. It is an unauthorized assumption, promulgated under circumstances unfavorable to dispassionate inquiry, that henceforth the narrower view alone shall be tolerated, and the broader stamped out by ecclesiastical ostracism and censure.

There has been good reason for delay, but now with better reason we grapple the problem hopefully. Yet our induction, as in all broad questions of fact, requires the patient study of various conditions and a multitude of details. It must proceed slowly, reserving its definitions to the last.

It is said that several years before his death the late eminent and venerable ex-President Theodore Woolsey was solicited to prepare an article on inspiration for a leading quarterly. He positively declined, alleging the difficulty of the subject, and avowing his personal incompetency. He added that the time for successful effort in that direction had not yet come.

We cannot doubt that he expressed the feeling of many of those who are best qualified to deal with such mysteries. Yet, without the slightest misgiving, they have yielded their mind, heart, and will to the Scriptures as given by the inspiration of God. Such undoubting faith is not at all inconsistent with a confessed inability to explain the divine energy by which the result was produced. This has special reference to the phenomena of the earlier stages of revelation.

We may feel painfully that no theory has been propounded that relieves all the difficulties of the case, yet enjoy an unfaltering confidence that the Bible is the word of God. For our confidence does not depend upon human theories concerning its production, but upon many infallible proofs of the divine origin both of the Old Testament and of the New, and these intrinsic, wrought into their substance, and filling them with light, and life, and power.

Discussions have recently become rife in one of the largest and most influential bodies of Protestant

Christendom about the inerrancy of Scripture. It is between those who maintain the most literal verbal inspiration, on the one side, and on the other, those who hold to an inspiration in the thought rather than in the words, that produces results that are infallible in all matters of faith and practice, but which does not preclude inaccuracies in matters not affecting the substance of religious truth.

There is reason to believe that while the latter position is earnestly opposed by an apparent majority in the church referred to, there are not a few, still numbered with that majority, who have become convinced that the Bible contains some inaccuracies in connection with extra-religious and unimportant matters, but have not spoken out plainly. They cannot yet reconcile this view with their Confession of Faith, and utter the admission reluctantly and scarcely above their breath. They consider such an admission premature and injudicious, and heartily regret that entire silence upon the subject had not been maintained. They do not see their way to any statement of the doctrine of inspiration that recognizes the least error in the Bible without a dangerous concession to those who deny its divine authority, and serious disturbance to the simple faith that receives every minutest item in the sacred Book as perfect and infallible. While they are under the pressure of such doubt, we can scarcely wonder that they are intensely disturbed.

But it is too late for regrets. The issue has been raised and must be met without flinching. It imperatively demands all reasonable effort to furnish such defining and explanatory statements concerning the inspiration of prophets and apostles as shall fairly cover the facts that confront us in their writings.

It must be confessed that the principle of verbal inspiration has been inflexibly maintained by many of our representative men,—intelligent, conscientious, and entitled to the highest respect for their gracious qualities,—and that they have been in the majority. It is painful to resist them. But a change is going on before our eyes, and it must surely prevail. It is not a caprice, originating in fondness for novelty and change, but a legitimate and necessary onward step in sacred learning. It is the result of more exhaustive study of the Scriptures by improved critical and exegetical methods, leading to a more correct apprehension of their ruling principle and contents.

It should be noted, too, in this connection, that knowledge in all departments is characteristically progressive. This arises from the constitution of the human mind, and from the vastness of the fields to be explored on every side. The active intellect, having abundant material to work upon, must make continual acquisitions. There is no such thing possible, except with fossils whose organic life is a thing of the by-gone ages, as settling down in contentment with the past, as if the utmost limit of attainment had been reached. Most of all, steady advance may be expected in divine knowledge, the partial ever becoming more perfect, and with every ascent to higher truth, the horizon expanding illimitably, and inviting to fresh toil, in order that still loftier heights may be surmounted.

It may further be observed among these prefatory generalities, that an important step forward is seldom, if ever, simultaneous on the part of the great mass, as if moved by a common impulse. Usually an individual explorer makes a discovery, and another here, and another there, all of like drift and bearing. At first a very few will grasp and accept the conclusion in which his alleged facts converge, perhaps with some necessary modifications, where the ardor of successful inquiry has carried the explorer too far. As the proof of its correctness becomes more convincing, others and still others will join in, until the new truth has become established as part of the sum of human knowledge.

There is always, and it is well that there should be, in order that hasty generalizations and rash conclusions may be avoided, a cautious conservative element, that clings fondly and tenaciously,—often too fondly and tenaciously,—to the old ; that resists vigorously,—often, but not always, wisely,—all abandonment of positions previously occupied.

It is unquestionable that sometimes strong and cultivated minds tend toward ultra-conservatism. Conservatism within bounds is wholesome, and serviceable to truth in restraining ardent and too credulous natures. As to extreme conservatism and extreme progressiveness, it is hard to say which is the more harmful. If we must have either, it is well that we should have its opposite as a necessary counterbalancing force. Sound, sober, and unbiassed judgment will find the truth somewhere between them. This remark would not be entitled to a place here if it did not seem applicable to present theological differences.

II.

VERBAL OR PLENARY INSPIRATION.

The conception of those who believe in the inerrancy of all the contents of the Bible, implies a divine energy that so completely absorbs and controls the human composer, as to ensure absolute truth in the most unimportant details, rendering the slightest inaccuracy impossible. If this assumption be warranted, a denial of the flawless perfection of these records, or of any part of them, is impugning the truthfulness of God.

The argument is *a priori*, and very simple and intelligible. It is held to be so conclusive that any attempt to test its soundness by critical examination is scarcely less than profane. Let the reasoning be approved, and the verbal inspiration of the Scriptures becomes virtually axiomatic. No evidence to the contrary is entitled to the slightest consideration. On this principle the actual must be forced into conformity with the theoretical, and facts that present opposition have a prospect before them of torture and suffering.

With respect to apparent inaccuracies, it is contended that the text may have been accidentally or intentionally corrupted,—or some other satisfactory explanation will be discovered, as often before in cases of alleged error,—and that at all hazards, without admitting the shadow of a doubt, the original text must be maintained, infallible and unexceptionable to the letter. "Let God be true and every man a liar."

We are reminded of a fierce controversy that raged more than two centuries ago between mighty chieftains in Biblical philology, about the Greek of the New Testament. The contending parties were called respectively Purists and Hellenists. The former claimed that the language of this highest inspiration must have been the most perfect of its kind—classic Greek of the purest type. How could the all-perfect God in communicating with men employ a medium so far below the highest standard as deservedly to be branded as corrupted and impure?

The opponents of this *a priori* theory simply appealed to facts. They examined the words and phrases of the New Testament, and exhibited their prevailing correspondence, not with Greek of the golden, classic age, but with Jewish contemporaries of the New Testament writers, who borrowed their constructions, idioms, and forms from their native Hebrew; whose finest models are found in the Old Testament Scriptures. This Greek, as compared with the language of Homer, Herodotus, and Demosthenes, must be pronounced corrupt.

It hardly needs to be mentioned which party had the best of it. Who cannot see now a wondrous providential wisdom by which a language was prepared in which the divine thoughts of a new revelation, that depended on Hebrew prophets and bards for its germinal principles and its grandest conceptions of a God unknown to the sages of Greece, could be more adequately expressed than by the finest Greek that ever vibrated upon the human ear? That splendid language in its earlier and purer form, with all the wealth of its vocabulary, could not give utterance to the thoughts that were now to enlighten the world. But as modernized, or even vulgarized and corrupted, in the mongrel Hellenistic Greek, it was more perfectly adapted to the gracious purposes of God and the needs of men. The illustration has a bearing upon our present line of thought which we need not more distinctly exhibit.

An apparent majority in the recent discussions esteem the Scriptures of the Old and New Testaments, all of them equally, to be the inspired and inerrant word of God for all the world and for all time, as truly as if they had come immediately from God, word by word, without human intervention. Yet the idea of verbal inspiration in the more mechanical sense, regarding the writers as mere amanuenses, has been generally abandoned. It is now freely admitted that differences in style and in modes of expression that exhibit individuality, forbid the thought of their writing, as if from dictation, by the injection of words apart from any normal intellectual process of their own.

The substituted conception is called by preference *Plenary Inspiration*. It is that the unerring divine wisdom takes possession of the prophet and controls every activity of his mind and heart, and that its expression of truth is human only in form—nay, more, that its form is absolutely, though mediately, determined in every syllable and letter. For it is held that indirectly, through the medium of human faculties, yet no less truly, the words are produced by the inspiring power. They are consequently of immutable significance and value, and infallible through all time as a directory for thought and conduct.

If the *a priori* argument be valid this ideal perfectness, quite apart from any thought of the intrinsic importance of a given record, is unquestionable. All personal deficiency in the prophet must have been miraculously supplied. There can be no failure of memory or lack of information, philosophical or scientific, geographical or historical. There can occur neither solecism nor anachronism—no inapt quotation or illustration, no dialectic flaw, and scarcely a rhetorical infelicity.

Must this beautiful conception, which anchors the soul fast to permanent and unchangeable truth, and excludes every blemish from the Scriptures, be abandoned or even modified? We answer, however reluctantly, that it must surely be put aside, unless it corresponds with the observed fact, and is confirmed by other than *a priori* reasoning. Yet the questioner has the right to ask, what new discoveries require the modification, and enable us to describe the inspiration of the Scriptures more intelligently?

It is the point toward which without solicitation we

are steadily pressing. But there can be no idealizing here. Our conclusion must be well considered, and founded upon a broad induction of facts. The problem to be solved requires imperatively the careful, dispassionate examination of the writings that have come to be accepted as having their origin in the inspiration of God. This can only be properly accomplished by men of acute and honest minds, and thoroughly trained for their work. It must, too, have extended over sufficient time to admit of the revision of hasty judgment, and the abandonment of hypotheses not supported by adequate evidence.

Yet the time need not be immeasurably protracted, inasmuch as a discovery of inaccuracies in any appreciable degree must compel us to revise our theory of inspiration, if it be one that requires absolute inerrancy. Neither should we ignore whatever labor has been already expended in this investigation. Indeed, we distinctly claim that facts have already been discovered that discredit the exactness of statement so earnestly affirmed, and that enable those who scoff at supernatural revelation to work with terrible effect in gathering into their own camp those not thoroughly grounded in the Christian faith, and even in unsettling many who thought themselves upon sure ground. It is the deep conviction of this that has impelled—or we might say compelled—the preparation of these pages. There may be infinite peril in refusing to strengthen our position, if we find that which we have hitherto occupied to be no longer tenable. Or even, like honest men, if it be fairly proven that the inspiration of the Bible is a delusion, at whatever sacrifice of cherished hope, let us know the truth.

It is not apt to occur to those who without difficulty maintain their souls in stalwart and unflinching faith, that a solution of moral paradoxes, or of apparent incongruities and contradictions, that is wholly satisfactory to themselves and to others of like proclivities and prepossessions, may be of little value to those who tend in the opposite direction. Elaborate and ingenious explanations and replies may be absolutely conclusive to the one class, whose souls are at rest, unconsciously predisposed to accept any plausible statement in reply to an objector, yet may be perfectly irrelevant and worthless to the other—and this other often includes men of earnest soul, who would give the world to feel their feet standing upon solid ground. The former are in no peril. They have usually an inward ground of certainty, which is quite independent of questions that touch only the surface of divine truth. It is the latter class, sinking into depths of darkness and despair, whom we would gain, if possible, for truth and for God.

It may be said triumphantly, as if this ought to silence all questioning, that it cannot be demonstrated that *the original text* contained a single error, and that the Bible, as we have it, may have been variously mutilated by carelessness or ignorance in transcribers or editors. But how weak in such a matter is a negation or a merely possible conjecture. And what if some of these almost frantic ones prefer to accept the conclusions of many eminent, candid, and patient Christian scholars, and honestly believe that it has been demonstrated, or, at least, is beyond reasonable doubt, that even as they came from the hands of their original penmen, the books were not immaculate? Receiving from the church its idea of inspiration as necessarily perfect, they must believe that a single ascertained error vitiates the whole —that if the Book is not infallible in all its parts, containing the truth, the whole truth, and nothing but the truth, it is not divine—that we can have no Bible, if not an inerrant Bible. Alas, for the poor souls whose last hope of finding God is thus blasted. By the cogent arguments of one body of distinguished Christian teachers, they are compelled to believe that no book that contains any error can be divinely inspired. By another equally distinguished and trustworthy group, they are assured that the Bible contains many errors. So, under the alternate guidance of great Biblical leaders, they pass off into the outer darkness.

Surely it is time for an adjustment, a reconstruction —time to find some new ground in defending the Scriptures against the assaults of scepticism. This must come, if at all, from understanding them better ourselves.

III.

INSPIRATION AND THE EARLIER BIBLICAL STUDY.

WHAT did the sagacious Christian scholar mean, who declined to grapple with the subject of inspiration on the ground of his personal incompetence? He must have been convinced that the current definitions, for reasons which he did not state, were no longer satisfactory—that embarrassments had arisen, in view of which, at least for the present, the task of preparing a reliable substitute, was too great for him. Nothing less than a fresh inspiration would suffice.

And what did the good Dr. Woolsey feel in the air —what sign of the times did he discern—that warranted his half prophecy of a better time coming, perhaps not very far off, when inspiration should be better understood, and attempts at definition might be undertaken more hopefully? His "*not yet*" is very significant.

He must have referred, as essential to success, to more careful, dispassionate, and exhaustive study of the Bible, in order that all the data for an intelligent estimate of the nature of inspiration might be obtained. He was aware that such study was being prosecuted with intense enthusiasm by competent men. It was all the better for the sake of fairness, and of sound conclusions, that the friends and the foes of supernatural religion were engaged with like diligence in winnowing the mass, searching for facts that might be helpful in solving the problems of the wonderful Book.

We are glad to believe that President Woolsey saw influences at work that were clearing the way for an intelligent view of inspiration—one that should bring relief to minds harassed by doubt, and fast tending toward absolute scepticism, — a consummation devoutly to be wished for, the great desideratum of the present stage of religious advance. Of what consequence is the settlement of theological differences on the minor details of our Christian faith in comparison with this?

The first thing we have to do in order to justify as not premature an attempt to penetrate the mystery of inspiration, as far as is possible under our finite limitations, is to give some description of the progress and present status of Biblical science, in its bearing upon the subject under consideration.

We must begin with the period of the Reformation, tracing rapidly the course and results of theological research in connection with the Bible, out of which have grown the contrary opinions that are now distracting us. We shall then understand how the more rigid view of inspiration, that is now being pressed, as belonging to the marrow of orthodoxy in the Presbyterian sense, has obtained its firm hold upon many minds, even while to all appearance it was an open question whether inspiration is in the letter or in the substance—whether it is verbal or conceptual.

We shall also discover by what discipline an impression just as deep and strong has been produced upon others, and for the best reasons is steadily gaining ground, that the former view is erroneous and must be essentially modified.

It is a phase of the subject that has not yet come to the surface with sufficient distinctness in the recent agitation, that the rival conceptions of inspiration are connected respectively with the two principal types of theological acquisition whose material lies before us in the Scriptures,—Systematic and Biblical Theology. This important circumstance places us under the necessity in connection with our subject of examining them carefully in their inception and distinguishing characteristics.

The Biblical work of the reformers was multifarious. Principally it was expository. They knew nothing of the refinements of exegetical science. These belonged to the unexplored future. With vigorous intellect and divinely illuminated, they unfolded the saving truth of the Scriptures to the people, who needed and craved the knowledge of which they had been deprived by priestly despotism. It was dealing out the bread of life to the famishing. Their expositions were in a measure controversial, but only so far as to deliver the consciences of men from the sophistries that enslaved them.

As they found occasion they exhibited the distinctive features of the various sacred writings, and inci-

THE EARLIER BIBLICAL STUDY. 19

dentally said what seemed necessary of their authorship, inspiration, and divine authority. No theory of verbal inspiration hampered them, for they sometimes separated themselves from traditional opinions on these subjects. But their treatment of such matters was not scientific, and they made no attempt to cover the whole ground of Biblical Introduction or any of its parts.

As for the Textual Criticism of the Old and New Testaments, it received early attention from men of high scholarly attainments. It is not necessary to dwell on it here. Most manuals introductory to the study of the Bible furnish a sufficient account of all that was done in the correction of the sacred text during the Reformation period, and of all thereafter down to the present time. This was the work of specialists in the original languages of the Bible.

The free study of the Scriptures in connection with reformation work naturally developed differences of opinion about matters not fundamental. The Bible was agreed upon with entire unanimity as the divine rule of faith, proclaiming pardon and acceptance with God only through believing in Christ as crucified for sin. But the same statement of doctrine upon minor points was not acceptable to all. During a protracted period the labors of theologians most competent to such work were principally directed to shaping methodical formularies, the Creeds and Confessions of Protestant Christendom. These summaries of doctrine in their logical arrangement constitute the basis of Systematic Theology. They embody the condensed substance of the Biblical study of the reformers, of which Systematic Theology is the expansion.

The craftsmen employed in this branch of theological discipline were able and laborious, but their system was mechanical and artificial. Its outline was constructed on strictly logical principles, resembling in character and method the work of the mediæval schoolmen. Its divisions and subdivisions were arranged with admirable symmetry and precision. Careful definitions and abundant explanatory and dialectic statements prepared the way for citations from Scripture. Each successive point must have its proof text, perhaps several. For a century or two theological thought was largely absorbed in detaching fragments from the mass of inspired material. After these had been kneaded and perhaps softened by the heat of controversy into a condition plastic enough for such a purpose, they were pressed into the moulds which accurate and artistic manipulation, partly mechanical and partly metaphysical, had prepared for them. The labor of these systematizers was like the toil of the bees storing the sweets they have gathered into the cells previously constructed on the scientific principles implanted in bee-nature from the beginning. So these painstaking theologians improved each shining hour according to the capacities and limitations that were theirs by heredity and training. Yet they did not and could not claim that their work, like that of the bees, was perfect of its kind. The material has often been recast. By successive efforts the divine doctrines have been more lucidly stated, more ingeniously adjusted, and more thoroughly fortified at every point where weakness was discovered.

The principal improvement in later elaborations arises from the advance in exegetical science during the last fifty years. But the authors of many of the ablest theological text-books, which are still appealed to as great authorities, were not accomplished in exegesis. Their citations were often made without the slightest regard to their setting or connection in the Sacred Volume, as usually determining the thought in the writer's mind. A close examination on sound hermeneutical principles often exhibits a meaning quite different from that assumed by the dogmatician. Now and then they dash upon any form of words in the current version of the Bible that seems pertinent, and the student must find in the exegetical room a corrective for the errors of his system.

But whatever improvement has been made in the method of imparting a comprehensive knowledge of the contents of Scripture, its ruling presupposition remains the same. The working hypothesis in Systematic Theology is that of verbal inspiration, uniform in perfectness and value from beginning to end. This is not only incorporated in its definitions, but exhibited in all its details. A disposition is now most manifest to cling to it with the utmost tenacity and exclusiveness, as if the slightest weakness at this point were a fatal concession to the opponents of supernatural revelation. The question is, whether this hypothesis can stand before the freer and more exhaustive investigation to which we have been constrained by irresistible forces from within and without.

We shall presently give more thought to this branch of ministerial training. But we can already see very clearly in what connection the principal difficulty in securing general acceptance for any other view of inspiration will probably be found.

IV.

TWO THEOLOGIES IN CONTRAST.

We are ready now for a postponed question. If the simple view of inspiration that anchors the soul fast to the inerrant, permanent, and unchangeable truth, must be exchanged for some other, what new discoveries require the exchange, and enable us to describe the inspiration of the Scriptures more intelligently?

The answer to this question is found in a more thorough acquaintance with the character and import of these Scriptures as exhibited in Biblical Theology, with the aid of the indispensable adjunct, the Higher Criticism.

We might ask, as a counter question to the above, whether the inquirer is sure that divine communications, through an inspired prophet, recorded in the Bible, always exhibit perfect, permanent, and unchangeable truth, and are never, as imperfect and unworthy to endure, modified and superseded in adaptation to improved conditions at a subsequent time.

One would suppose that the ready unanimity with which we agree that the Levitical worship has been thus superseded, should prepare us for other changes on the same principle. It is a hint for the future. Its ground will appear more distinctly as we advance.

It is important to state here more fully what these sciences are, for the benefit of those who scarcely know them except as names, yet are deeply interested in discussions that relate to the inerrancy of Scripture and the nature of inspiration. It should be known that they are indeed sciences, and that their principles and contents are of great value in their bearing upon our present subject of thought.

Until within the last twenty-five years Biblical Theology has been almost unknown except by those fully acquainted with the theological literature of Germany. Systematic, sometimes called Dogmatic or Didactic Theology, previously held an exclusive position in the orderly exhibition of divine truth. The title of neither indicates very sharply the distinction between them, for either designation is in some degree descriptive of both methods, the Systematic and the Biblical.

They agree in finding in the Scriptures a comprehensive and reliable statement of the facts and principles of God's moral administration in the earth—a spiritual religion, embracing all the material for the education of our higher nature, and relatively perfect in its wise adaptation to the condition and needs of men during their earthly existence. It follows that Systematic Theology is Biblical, as well as the so-called Biblical.

The two Theologies also agree in recognizing a relation between the truths of the Bible, and that they can only be adequately apprehended in their mutual bearings and interdependence; and each method has its framework and principle of coherence. It follows that Biblical Theology is systematic, as well as the so-called Systematic.

But as already intimated the *framework* of Systematic Theology is artificial and scholastic, rather than Biblical. It distributes the contents of the Bible into general heads, and then by logical gradation descends from generals to particulars. It is pre-eminently scientific and symmetrical, but cold, metaphysical, abstract, and lifeless. It assumes that the whole truth is known upon every subject, and can be stated with such precision and accuracy in definitions, theses, and dialectic formulæ, that it can be fully apprehended by faculties capable of mastering any other systems of science or philosophy.

Systematic Theology is Biblical, but it treats the Bible as a heterogeneous mass of religious truth, its elements indiscriminately commingled, and requiring severe and accomplished critical sagacity,—a purely intellectual process,—in order to bring its statements into some intelligible order and coherence under the most approved methods of classification. It gives scope to the finest and most subtle tact and ingenuity in filling up inferentially any chasms that may be discovered, in removing excrescences, or, at least, smoothing them down so that they shall not repulsively obtrude, in reconciling apparent contradictions, and in furnishing shrewd replies to objections from whatever source they may emanate.

The truth is thus introduced to the world in good form, that is, truth as estimated by the theologian and his circle. It commends itself to cultured intellect as worthy of all respect, and entitled to a distinguished place among the sciences into which the sum of human knowledge is distributed.

Moreover, it has long stood approved as an indispensable part of the scholastic cultivation to which the minds of the professional conservators and expounders of divine truth must be subjected before they are qualified for their office. Every minute point in theology is in its right place, and the system can be easily memorized, and always held ready for use upon suitable occasion. The young man who has fully mastered his system of Didactic and Polemic Theology has a complete outfit. If properly husbanded, it may last him for a lifetime. As a warrior in the ranks of the church militant, he can never be put to shame before the adversary.

The term *Biblical Theology* was first used as the title of a book in 1792 by C. F. Ammon, a rationalist. His view is without vitality or coherence, and based on no discriminating definition. It entirely disregards the suggestion of Gäbler five years earlier, that it is the historic principle that distinguishes Biblical Theology from Dogmatic. Moreover, it is far less Biblical than the scholasticism against whose inexorable logic it rebels.

Various theories, verging more and more toward a correct conception, were propounded during the next forty years by L. Baur, Kaiser, De Wette, and others.

The mythical hypothesis of Strauss in his "Life of Jesus," and the "tendency" theory of F. Baur, the father of the Tübingen Theology, called forth the masterly replies of Neander in his "Planting and Training of the Christian Church" (1832), an important step in advance. It is based on a sound historic criticism of the New Testament writings, the principle of which is easily carried over to the Old. It is that of a normal historical development of divine truth, in a series of successive revelations. The course and order of this development are ascertained by the careful examination of the inspired writings in the fundamental conception of each, and in their mutual relations as essential parts of a harmonious and consistent whole.

It is in the "Biblical Theology of the New Testament," by C. F. Schmid (Tübingen, 1853), and the post-humous "Theology of the Old Testament," by G. F. Oehler (Tübingen, 1873), that the subject first receives a definition and treatment that establish its claim to be recognized as a special and independent training. They understand by Biblical Theology, the historico-genetic presentation of revealed religion in the canonical writings of the Old and New Testaments. They distinguish it from Systematic Theology by its historical character, while by its limitation to the canonical writings of the Old and New Testaments, it is separated from Historical Theology, and characterized as an integral part of Exegetical Theology. These discriminations by Schmid are of great importance.

Biblical Theology has its beginning and source in patient and thorough exegetical training and labor. Its exegesis is historico-grammatical, but always with due regard to the unity, and living coherence and symmetry that distinguish a progressive revelation of divine wisdom, grace, and power in connection with sin and redemption. It is important to notice that it embraces, not only didactic utterances, abstract announcements of truth, but persons, events, institutions, and the whole concrete substance of history in connection with the divine administration of human affairs.

Biblical Theology, in pursuance of its historic principle, follows the order of revelation in the Sacred Books. It presents truth, not in preconceived logical combinations, but in accordance with the general development required for the education of man in the successive stages of his existence upon the earth. It begins with the rudiments of knowledge, and advances step by step in successive disclosures, adapting itself to a growing capacity in men for the apprehension of the highest truth, and ever tending toward the culmination of God's grace in a completed redemption.

Revelation, as considered by this science, keeps pace with Providence and the course of human events as divinely directed, as well as with the intellectual and moral advancement of its subjects. Hence Biblical Theology takes careful note, as part of its material, not only of inspired communications, the words of God through the mouth of a prophet, but as above stated, of everything connected with the divine ordering of human affairs by which men might attain a fuller knowledge of God, and their purposes and conduct might be swayed in the right direction.

It will thus be seen that Biblical Theology regards the matter of revelation, not abstractly, as made up of certain logical propositions to be proved and maintained by the most conclusive dialectic methods, the substance and sinew of an inspired System of Theology, but concretely, as wrought by the divine Spirit into human existence, individual and social, and adapting itself to all varieties of character, condition, and circumstances that diversify the race.

In Biblical Theology the truth, as embodied in the Sacred Books in facts and events more than in words, is a living organism that separates from everything extraneous to itself. It exhibits the Old Testament and the New, with all their coherences and contrasts, as parts of a great whole, and the relation between them as not accidental, nor arbitrary, nor mechanical, but natural, necessary, and vital.

Its central idea and ruling principle, its inspiration, is the development of a gracious purpose of God pertaining to the salvation of the human race as a fact in the course of accomplishment. The science which treats the divine revelation in the Scriptures most philosophically and correctly, and with the clearest discernment of its grandeur, is that which follows the course and order of its expansion from a feeble beginning till its full glory is realized in the ultimate triumph of the grace and righteousness of God over all evil in the ascension glory of Christ.

We have precious material in this whole description for our promised reconstruction. It must surely be remembered in our *a posteriori* definition, toward which by easy stages we are moving forward.

V.

THE HIGHER CRITICISM, DESTRUCTIVE AND CONSTRUCTIVE.

BIBLICAL THEOLOGY is a growth. It is becoming more and more a strong, beautiful, and fruitful growth. It is mainly the product of two living forces, that have been vigorously at work for years. They are Biblical Exegesis and the Higher Criticism.

The three are inseparable, and have matured co-ordinately. Their advance has been quickened and determined by the activity of opposing forces against which they have combined.

It will be understood that it was for the assailants of revealed truth to choose their point of attack, to which its defenders must necessarily accommodate themselves. Wherever an onset is made, the repelling force must be rallied. Every thrust must be at once warded off by the quickly advanced shield and buckler. Every mine must be met by a counter-mine. Every sophism must be exposed, and annihilated by sound logic. Every misrepresentation must be nullified by correct statement.

Those who read the Bible devoutly as part of their religious discipline, finding in it strength and salvation, but who can spare no time from their daily pursuits for its careful study, are not usually aware what fierce battles have been fought over every inch of the surface. To them it is all holy ground. They come to some rough places, to some things that are unintelligible, to some early records that seem inconsistent with the spirit and substance of the Gospel. But not willing to be perplexed, they do not dwell upon them anxiously. They find some relief in remembering that the statements in question are connected with long past conditions, and were not intended for their guidance. It is enough for them that they see throughout the whole mass of writings the footprints of the Almighty, and they are content to leave everything doubtful to be cleared up by the brighter light of the future. Taken as a whole, what they find here is sacred and delightful.

The battle with the destructive school in its various branchings began with its adoption of a false exegesis. As a first and ruling principle it discredited all statements that involve the supernatural. There were the 'accommodation theory' of Semler, the 'moral interpretation' of Kant, the 'naturalistic view' of Paulus, the 'mythical hypothesis' of Strauss, the 'tendency theory' of Baur, and the arbitrary assumptions of Schenkel and Rénan. All of these are rationalistic, and each urged its claim to reception as a satisfactory solution of the alleged monstrosities of the Bible.

Their attacks were repelled by advancing against them sound exegetical principles. An important result of the contest was the discovery and adoption of right methods in interpreting Scripture. Every word and phrase must be carefully scrutinized, and its meaning determined in accordance with the linguistic use of its own time in the evolutionary development of language.

More and more fully the historico-grammatical system of exegesis in its application to the Scriptures, was exhibited and adopted. It held as a primary conception, that always, in endeavoring to understand the meaning of an author, due regard must be paid to the unity and living coherence of a progressive revelation.

By this matured and impregnable exegetical science the great chasm that separates us from those who "spake as they were moved by the Holy Ghost" in very ancient times, is bridged over. In imagination we place ourselves among them. We learn to think as they thought, to speak as they spoke, to consider everything in their circumstances, history, and intellectual or moral culture, that would affect their modes of thought and speech. It is only when we have done this that we can fairly understand them.

Here came in the Higher Criticism, known long before by another designation. It is imperative in Biblical Theology that everything embraced in the writings that constitute its material should be assigned, as nearly as possible, to the right time and place. Until this is done the exegetical process, as above described, cannot be completed.

The Higher Criticism has most to do with the human element in the Bible. It considers questions of age, authorship, genuineness, and canonical authority. It traces the origin, preservation, and integrity of the various books, and exhibits their scope, contents, relations, and general character and value.

Thus by the closest and most patient examination of these writings, on such scientific principles as are commonly applied to very ancient books, each several portion comes to be duly appreciated and fitted into its right place in relation to other revelation. The more general and older name of this science is *Isagogics*, or *Biblical Introduction*. It is called the Higher Criticism to distinguish it from Textual Criticism, which only seeks to ascertain the exact words of the original Scriptures.

More recent investigations in the Higher Criticism have excited the strongest prejudice in many, as if new and graceless methods had been introduced by men in close sympathy with the destructive criticism of the Bible. They regard it as imperilling everything holy and precious in revealed religion, and fervently desire that it could be banished into oblivion.

They surely are not aware how actively and craftily the enemies of their faith are using the Higher Criticism, and have long been using it, in undermining the fabric of revelation. The grandest efforts in this same Higher Criticism, followed by the most important results in the establishment of correct principles, were compelled by the spurious conjectural criticism of Spinoza, a renegade Jew and Pantheist, who anticipated by nearly two centuries the teachings of the later rationalists, and the untenable theories of Richard Simon, Clericus, and Semler.

In reply to these Du Pin, Witsius, Prideaux, Vitringa, and Calmet laid the foundations of legitimate historical inquiry into the origin, character, and value of the Sacred Writings. These were followed in the same field by the Abbe Fleury, Astruc, Bishop Lowth, and the poet Herder.

The products of their labors in the accumulation of facts and the discovery of right principles, prepared the way for the comprehensive work of J. G. Eichhorn in 1780, who has justly been styled the father of the Higher Criticism. Under the more general name Biblical Introduction, important contributions to the science have been made by the English and American scholars, T. H. Horne, Moses Stuart, Edward Robinson, S. H. Turner, Samuel Davidson, and others.

In 1862 new interest in the subject was roused by the attack of Bishop Colenso on the historical character of the Old Testament writings, and by the rationalism of the authors of "Essays and Reviews." These called forth able and conclusive replies on both sides of the Atlantic. Since then the German Wellhausen and the Hollander Kuenen, in the spirit of Colenso, have compelled fresh efforts to maintain the credibility and authority of the Old Testament Scriptures against the assaults of rationalism.

In Great Britain and America, the constructive Higher Criticism, now becoming reconstructive, seems to be dividing itself between the more progressive, represented by Bishop Lightfoot, Drs. W. Robertson Smith, Briggs, Cheyne, Driver, Harper, Brown, and others, and those less willing to accept advanced views, headed by Dr. W. Henry Green, with a large following, especially in his own branch of Protestantism. Whatever may be the further outcome of their investigations and discussions, truth cannot suffer at their hands.

It is too late to decry the Higher Criticism, or to deny that it is a field of research on which have been won the noblest triumphs in behalf of the supreme authority of the Scriptures as embodying a divine revelation, over the destructiveness of rationalism.

VI.

MINOR INACCURACIES.

WE postpone for the present a further consideration of the result of these labors in a more complete and illuminative Biblical Theology. It will come in its place.

We have now reached the most ungracious part of our task—that of mentioning inaccuracies in the Bible which make it necessary to reconstruct the theory of inspiration as generally accepted.

It will be sufficient to adduce a few out of the multitude of instances in which human infirmity is apparent. For the definition referred to as untenable, claims absolute inerrancy and faultless perfection for the whole.

With respect to inerrancy, whether of the received or the original text, the Old Testament is far more questionable than the New. But even in the New Testament inaccuracies occur, to which the following description of Professor Green, and which he virtually admits, will certainly apply: "They are in the *minima* of Scripture, in trivialities that are of no account, and neither disparage the truthfulness of the narrative, nor in any way affect its doctrinal statements; and which are compared by Dr. Charles

Hodge ('Systematic Theology,' vol. i., p. 170) to 'the specks of sandstone here and there in the marble of the Parthenon.'"

Of this trivial character is the citation in Matt. xxvii. 9 of a passage from Zech. xi. 12, 13, giving Jeremiah as its author. A simple lapse of memory, utterly unimportant.

Such, too, is the discrepancy between Matt. xx. 29, 30, and Luke xviii. 35. In the former we have two blind men crying after Jesus as He *went out from* Jericho, in the latter of one blind man as he *drew nigh to* that city.

Similarly trivial is the difference between the Gospels about the hour of the crucifixion, and scarcely more important, that between John and the Synoptical Gospels with regard to the time of the last Passover. If we can reconcile them, it is well; but if not, we need not be disturbed.

Even in the discourses of our Lord, where as a rule we find far more exact verbal agreement than in the narrative portion of the Gospels, there is sometimes a difference in language, where the forms of expression they severally employ are not precisely equivalent, but a slight difference in thought is conveyed.

Here, also, belong the linguistic inaccuracies sketched in the following extract from the late Dr. Alexander McClelland's "Manual of Interpretation" (pp. 61–63). One who received from that distinguished teacher more than fifty years ago his instruction in the rudiments of Hebrew, and his earliest training in Criticism, Hermeneutics, and Exegesis, may be excused if he finds pleasure in giving the quotation here:

"Language is not the invention of metaphysicians or convocations of the wise and learned. It is the common blessing of mankind, formed for their mutual advantage in their intercourse with each other. Its laws are popular, not philosophical, being founded on the laws of thought which govern the whole mass in the community. . . . . Scarcely will we hear in a long and serious discourse between the best speakers a sentence which does not need some modification or limitation, in order that we may not attribute to it more or less than was intended. Nor is the operation at all difficult. We make the correction instantly, with so little cost of thought that we would be tempted to call it instinct, did we not know that many of our perceptions that seem to be intuitive, are the results of habit and education. It would be an exceedingly strange thing if the Bible, the most popular of all books, composed by men for the most part taken from the multitude, addressed to all, and on subjects interesting to all, were found written in language to be interpreted on different principles. But in point of fact it is not. Its style is eminently and to a remarkable degree that which we would expect to find in a volume designed by its author to be the people's book—abounding in all those kinds of inaccuracy which are sprinkled through ordinary discourses, hyperboles, analogues, and loose catachrestical expressions, whose meaning no one mistakes, though their deviation from the _plumb_ occasionally makes the small critic sad."

These are what Professor Green calls "the *minima*, trivialities, that neither disparage the truthfulness of the narrative, nor in any way affect the statement of doctrine." But who does not see that the admission of error, however comparatively unimportant, is fatal to the hypothesis of absolute inerrancy? They are unconscious mistakes, variations from the absolute truth, although as is claimed, they are no larger compared with the glorious substance of the revelation than the tiniest grains of sand in the marble of the Parthenon, as compared with the whole massive pile. But *degrees* of imperfection are not in question here. The mistakes are such as a human narrator might make most innocently. But divine authorship in the absolutely controlling sense that is asserted, must exclude even the least of them. In the matter of error, however harmless, the *a priori* theory admits of no *maxima* and *minima*.

That the Books of the Old Testament are inspired is proved mainly by our Saviour's endorsement of the Jewish Canonical Books. He continually quotes from them as fulfilled in himself, as worthy of all confidence, as diligently to be searched for testimony to his coming and glory. We shall not examine the sentences in which absolute endorsement is thought to be expressed, in order to ascertain whether they bind us to a strictly verbal inspiration of all the Scriptures. It is more than doubtful.

It only needs to be said for the present, that in our Lord's frequent reference to the Old Testament, verbal accuracy is practically treated as not of the slightest consequence. He refers constantly to translations in common use among the Jews, never hinting that their value is impaired by erroneous rendering; although very often, and in important places, they go very far astray from what could be the meaning of the original. The Septuagint version is much nearer to the Scriptures endorsed by our Saviour and his apostles than the received Hebrew text; for they generally quote from the former, and only occasionally from the Hebrew, or from some Aramaic version which in the Gospels is translated into Greek.

It cannot properly be inferred from this that the Greek translation was better than the Hebrew, and is to be substituted for it as the only inerrant Scripture. It simply means that truth as inspired by God is of such quality and nature that invariable verbal accuracy is not material. It may be expressed with great freedom and in various forms without impairing its substantial value. It is the thought that is inspired.

In turning to the Old Testament we are confronted by the fact that those who have most diligently engaged in the research that is needed to decide the question of inerrancy, the recognized specialists and adepts, the class of scholars properly looked to as authorities in historic and literary criticism,—whose competency, integrity, and absolute confidence in Old Testament revelation are unquestionable,—regard the insistance upon inerrancy in the inspired Scriptures as false in principle and in fact. Applying the scientific tests to these writings that are applied to other ancient literature, they find many inaccuracies and conflicting statements. Questions arise in these investigations on which individual opinions are of little worth, even of men eminent in intellect, learning, and love of truth, unless they are approved workmen in the line of study which entitles them to a hearing on matters of the kind. The dogmatist, the metaphysician, the etymologist, the rhetorician may each be treated with great deference in all that relates to his own special science. But as an authority for final decision in a case of great difficulty and importance, he must be kept within his own limits.

Let the circumstance be recalled from our preliminary statements, in view of which we are most anxious in maintaining the divine origin and authority of the Scriptures. It is that we are surrounded by an incomputable mass of unbelief of every shade and degree. In part, it is bold, defiant, even malignant, ready to see every weak point, and to use unscrupulously every advantage in confirming latent sceptical tendencies, and in gaining over those whose early faith in the Christian religion is becoming unsettled by philosophic, materialistic, or agnostic unbelief.

If it comes to be understood that it is the authoritative doctrine of the Church that the inspiration of the Scriptures depends upon the absolute immaculateness of the whole; and on the other hand, that a large proportion of those whose special scholarship qualifies them to speak decisively upon the subject admit that the Scriptures are not without error, and that they stand ready to prove it by many instances, we fear beyond measure the result.

MINOR INACCURACIES. 43

In fact the claim of Scripture infallibility in all historic and scientific details, where errors are visible to every eye, is making infidels by thousands.

Very clear and decisive upon this point is the language of the late Professor Evans: "You protest against the unsettling of faith. You do well. But they also do well who protest against keeping up needless barriers to faith. You condemn criticism which destroys belief in the Scriptures as the word of God. But beware of including in your condemnation the criticism which helps to make such belief in the Scriptures possible. You may be sure that so long as you hang the infallible authority of Scripture as the rule of faith on the infallible accuracy of every particular word and clause in the Book, as long as you exalt the Bible to the same pinnacle of authority in matters respecting which God has given us fuller and more exact revelations elsewhere, as in matters respecting which the Bible is the only revelation, the irrepressible conflict between faith and science will go on, and the Drapers and Whites of each generation will have their new chapters to add to the record. Every new discovery in science or in archæology that seems to contradict some particular statement will produce a panic. Every advance in criticism will tend to unsettle the faith of somebody whom your teaching has led to confound the form with the substance.

"This is a mistaken defence of Divine Revelation. Shipwrecks of faith without number have been caused by it. It is the very thing according to his own confessions that made an unbeliever of the most brilliant scholar of France, perhaps of the world to-day, Ernest Rénan. It is the very thing that drove into infidelity the strongest champion of the popular infidelity of England, who died the other day in his unbelief, Charles Bradlaugh. So testifies his own brother, a believer. But for this the iridescent declamation of Robert Ingersoll in his 'Mistakes of Moses,' would collapse like a pricked balloon. The Christianity of our day cannot afford to fight the battle of the Book on that line. It cannot afford to silence the larger, profounder, more Scriptural restatements of revealed truth made imperative by improved methods of Biblical research."

VII.

MINOR INACCURACIES—HISTORICAL.

Two instances of variations from fact in the Old Testament have been recently adduced by an accomplished Assyriologist.* The first is chronological. It is one out of many such embarrassments that occur in the Books of Kings.

It is in 2 Kings xxviii. 9, 10, where the chronological statement implies that Hezekiah began to reign 727 B.C.; for we know from Assyrian records that Samaria was taken in 722 B.C.

The difficulty lies in adjusting this record to the statement in verse 13: "Now in the fourteenth year of Hezekiah did Sennacherib, king of Assyria, come up against the fenced cities of Judah, and took them." There is scarcely any Assyrian campaign about which we are better informed from Assyrian sources than this campaign of Sennacherib. He made but one, and that took place 701 B.C. We are thus faced by a dilemma. Either 701 B.C. was the fourteenth year of Hezekiah, in which case he could not have commenced to reign in 727, or else he began to reign

---
* Professor Francis Brown, D.D.

727 B.C., in which case 701 was not his fourteenth year.

Of this the writer says: "Scholars differ as to the choice they make under these circumstances. . . . . Attempts to shake the date of Sennacherib's campaign have failed. As far as the material at our command permits us to go, the error was in the original document,—*i. e.*, is due to the responsible compiler of the Book of Kings, who wrote after the Northern Kingdom had for a hundred years or more ceased to exist, its people been deported or scattered, its records doubtless in large measure destroyed, and its territory largely given over to idolatry and semi-barbarism. I shall be grateful to any scholar who will give me light on this, as on other difficult questions of Biblical Chronology.

"But I refuse to shut my eyes to the fact of an apparent error, and I decline as a Christian man to connect my faith in my Redeemer, and in the revelation of God's love in him, in any way, shape, or manner with the dates of ancient Hebrew kings."

The second example given by the same writer is in the Book of Daniel. It relates to the statements in chap. v., with regard to affairs in Babylon after the reign of Nebuchadnezzar. He refers to various matters of complexity and difficulty. "But the difficulty reaches a climax in the mention of Darius the Mede (v. 31), who appears in the narrative to have been the immediate successor of Belshazzar, to have organized the empire (chap. vi.), to have been 'the son of Ahasuerus, of the seed of the Medes'

(ix. 1), and to have himself been succeeded by Cyrus the Persian (vi. 28). For this personage, cuneiform decipherment appears to have left no room. Perfectly explicit contemporary records do not permit a student of history any longer to doubt that Media fell before Babylon did; that the conqueror of Babylon was not a Mede, but a Persian ; that this conqueror was Cyrus, as the Old Testament elsewhere represents (*e. g.*, Isa xliv. 28, xiv. 1 ff., *cf.* xlvi. 1; 2 Chron. xxxvi. 22, 23=Ezr. i. 1–8); that his reign over Babylon was reckoned as beginning immediately upon the conquest, and that therefore no reign intervened between that of Nabonidus, the last Shemitic king, and his own ; that the only royal Darius known to history in that century, was not a Mede, but a Persian, not the son of Ahasuerus (Xerxes), but his father, not the predecessor of Cyrus, but a successor of his, according to the statement of Ezra iv. 5 : 'All the days of Cyrus, King of Persia, even until the reign of Darius, King of Persia'; in short, that as little as there is any place for Darius the Mede before Cyrus, just as little is there any extra-Biblical evidence that there was a Darius the Mede to take such a place; while there is strong evidence, such as historical students are bound to accept, and do accept, that there was not. The judgment expressed in the only commentary on the Book of Daniel, written in recent years by a scholar of competent equipment for the task—I refer to that of Meinhold, in the series of Strack and Zöckler—is in accordance with the weight of evidence : ' No Median sovereignty over Babylonia preceded the Persian, and Darius the Mede is not a historical figure.'

"I know that there is a great sensitiveness in some religious minds in regard to the Book of Daniel. I am sorry to disturb such minds. But it is indispensable that it should clearly be shown whither the extreme dogma that is claiming to be the sole orthodoxy is driving us. I am quite ready to grant that there are elements in the history of the third quarter of the sixth century B.C., which are not yet understood, and which may by some better understanding of them hereafter, enable us to see more distinctly the relations of various Bible statements; but from the point of view of historical scholarship, there is no reason to suppose that Darius the Mede will thereby be rehabilitated as an actual personage, any more than there is to expect the rehabilitation of the Sardanapalus and Semiramis of Greek legend. Even if that should occur, however, it remains true that no one who fairly weighs the facts as they at present appear, can say that they are favorable to the traditional opinion, and no one who loves the Bible can reflect without a shudder on the temerity of those who condition the fact and authority of divine revelation upon the slender possibility that the prevailing testimony of the credible witnesses to the facts may at some remote date be overthrown."

The above extracts are given because they are the latest instances of error in Biblical history that have been prominently mentioned, and are connected with the writer's very extensive examination of cuneiform tablets. Various explanations have been attempted of these, as of other apparent inaccuracies equally formidable, which, however, dispassionate and accomplished scholarship pronounces strained and improbable. Some of these are of such a nature that it is scarcely supposable that they should have resulted from the carelessness of a copyist, or that any one could have an object in altering the text intentionally.

It may be said that accidental or intentional alteration is in no case absolutely impossible. But as cases of extreme improbability multiply, the possibility that not one of the apparent errors were in the original text, becomes infinitesimal. Who must not regard with profound pity the anxious inquirer after saving truth, in its bearing upon his prospects for the life to come, who is informed that the truth of the Gospel as a revelation of divine mercy must be abandoned if the Old Testament or the New contains a single historic inaccuracy, however unimportant?

The recent discussions upon this subject in a branch of the American Church that embraces a larger number of devoted specialists in the Higher Criticism than any other, have raised an issue that can no longer be evaded. Whatever may be the ultimate action of that conservative body, the distinguished representative of conservatism who stands foremost, as entitled by his chosen line of study to speak as a specialist, stands nearly alone.

It is impossible to estimate what harm may result unless the whole subject be considered afresh, and some ground intelligibly stated upon which the inspiration of the Bible can be firmly and consistently maintained, without regard to occasional lapses of memory or defective information, which do not in the least affect the substance and gracious purpose of the revelation. We may well echo the exclamation of the writer last quoted against the temerity of suspending our faith in the Redeemer, and our eternal hope, upon the minute historical accuracy of every incident recorded in the Book of Genesis, or the Chronicles of the Kings of Judah.

We here quote with satisfaction the language of an anonymous writer describing a common misapprehension concerning the Higher Criticism in its purpose and results: "Many earnest and uncompromising Christians cannot see anything good in criticism. They arraign it as a foe to Christianity, and a would-be destroyer of the Bible. This is not at all strange; for the average man, untrained in historic criticism, cannot appreciate the nice discriminations of the critic. He wants a plain categorical statement, a simple alternative, with no possible middle ground, and no question left in suspense. He does not recognize the force of probable evidence, which in all departments of thought is the very guide of life. And least of all can he understand how a man can give up some views of the Bible without giving up the Bible itself. It is all or nothing with him. If he believes in the Bible at all, he believes in it as an infallible oracle, free from all errors and misstatements. And when criticism, which in its first touch is always destructive, like the frost, rejects a text

MINOR INACCURACIES—HISTORICAL. 51

here, gives a new meaning to a passage there, and throws over the whole volume a novel and strange atmosphere of naturalness, he cries out in wrath that the critics are trying to destroy the Bible.

"Such fear of criticism, however, does not belong to Christianity itself, but to its over-cautious defenders. As a matter of fact, the result thus far of Biblical Criticism has been to bring out more clearly the claims of the Bible to the regard of men. In innumerable ways the researches of the critics are confirming the veracity of the Bible, and investigation has left it in a much stronger, because more rational, position than it occupied before. Even the discrepancies and contradictions that criticism has discovered in it have confirmed its honesty and veracity, strange as it may appear. For they are just such discrepancies and contradictions as would be made by honest and truth-seeking men in the circumstances under which they wrote. For instance, there are two accounts given of the origin of the name Beer-sheba. In the twenty-first chapter of Genesis, we are told that it was so named by Abraham because of a striking event that happened there. And in the twenty-sixth chapter of the same book it is said that Isaac gave the place its name about ninety years later for a wholly different reason. Of course the harmonizers have tried to smooth over this difficulty, but with no success. The true explanation of this and many other contradictions of a similar character is that the Biblical writers and editors incorporated into their narrative accounts from different documents, and did not always notice the difference between these documents. This does not impeach the Bible as a record of God's dealings with men; but it does overthrow the theory that every word in it is infallibly inspired.

"The real enemy of the Bible is not the man who would test its claims by rules of legitimate and candid criticism, but the man who, by refusing to allow such tests, gives color to the belief that he fears the result. Christians of serene faith, who have caught the finer spirit of the religion of Christ, welcome all investigations and all tests, however disturbing may be their temporary effect."

Since the foregoing chapters were written we have examined with great interest an article by Professor W. Henry Green upon a difficult question of Old Testament Chronology.*

It is a comment upon the genealogies in Gen. v. and xi. The former of these records gives the line of descent from Adam to Shem, the latter thenceforward to Abraham. The Professor proposes to remove the conflict between the Biblical chronology and the conclusions of science with respect to the age of the world. That the scientific claim is imperative is sufficiently evident from the willingness to concede it manifested by so conservative a scholar.

We quote several leading sentences: "As mention is made of the age of each patriarch of the entire series at the birth of his son, it has been assumed that this supplies a basis for computing the length of time

---

* "Bibliotheca Sacra," April, 1890.

covered by these genealogies, and that it would be only necessary to add together the numbers thus given in order to ascertain the interval from Creation to the Flood, and from the Flood to the birth of Abraham. Estimates thus made out have been commonly accepted as the Biblical chronology of this primeval period, and the age of the world thus determined has been set over against the results of scientific investigation."

"I deny most emphatically," the writer goes on to say, "the antagonism, and the legitimacy of the assumption on which it rests. The author of these genealogies gives no intimation that they were constructed for any such purpose. He never puts them to this use himself. He nowhere sums these numbers, nor suggests their summation. No chronological statement is deduced from them, either by him or by any inspired writer. There is no computation anywhere in Scripture of the time that elapsed from the creation or from the deluge, as there is from the descent into Egypt to the Exodus (Ex. xii. 40), or from the Exodus to the building of the temple (1 Kings vi. 1). And if the numbers in these genealogies are for the sake of constructing a chronology, why are numbers introduced which have no possible relation to such a purpose? Why are we told how long each patriarch lived after the birth of his son, and what was the entire length of his life?"

The Professor makes room for the indefinite extension of time within the limits mentioned in the record, by suggesting that the Hebrew word "*begat*" may be used with equal propriety of an immediate or a remote descendant; and he cites several instances in which genealogies are constructed with the omission of some names, yet with no change in the word that expresses the connection. This usage is unquestionable. A notable instance is our Saviour's genealogy in the Gospel of Matthew.

But the proof from analogy unquestionably fails in there being no single genealogy on record which binds us fast at each successive step to an immediate descendant by mentioning the age of the father at the birth of the son. This mathematical precision forbids the supposition that in any instance the name given is not that of the progenitor's personal offspring, the nearest in descent,—that is, if historical accuracy is of the slightest importance.

But this is not all. The Professor must further assume that the genealogist has intentionally concealed his omission of one or more links in the chain, by substituting the name of the later descendant whom he chooses next to introduce, for that of the son actually born within the given limit of time. This involves a serious departure from historic fact.

Suppose, for illustration, that two more generations had been dropped from chapter xi.—those next after Arphaxad; omitting Shelah and Eber, and passing over to Peleg. If the text is altered to correspond in apparent exactness with the remainder of the chain, we must read by compression in verses 12–16: "And Arphaxad lived five and thirty years and begat Peleg. And Arphaxad lived after he begat Peleg four hundred and thirty years, and begat sons and daughters."

Now Peleg was at the nearest Arphaxad's great-grandson. If the genealogist has already omitted other generations at this point, the relationship must have been still more remote. But supposing the omission of only the two above mentioned names, Arphaxad must have been stated to be thirty-five years old at the birth of his great-grandson, and to have lived four hundred and thirty years thereafter.

We thus exemplify that according to the proposed theory the genealogy must contain at every omission of an immediate lineal descendant a palpable misstatement in respect to names, or figures, or both; and this by Moses, who is expressly mentioned in the article as undoubtedly the author. It involves the supposition that every error in figures has been adroitly covered up by a change in names, only to be discovered at this late period.

The esteemed writer was greatly perplexed, as many others have been before him, by the discrepancy between this genealogical record, in the only significance that has ever before been thought of as possible, and the fact ascertained by scientific research. But his ingenious proposition is an attempt to wrest asunder an iron chain, every link of which is thoroughly tempered and forged. It shows what bold expedients the Higher Criticism, if not too scrupulous, may resort to in dealing with the problems of the Bible. It is all in vain. The Hebrew terms that express relationship by descent are elastic. But there is no elasticity in mathematics.

The genealogical inaccuracy in Genesis remains. This brave effort only accentuates it, and we cannot hope that others will be more successful.

The same respected authority concedes a historic inaccuracy in Gal. iii. 17. It is in connection with Bishop Colenso's assertion of the impossibility of so large an Israelitish population as that given in Ex. xii. 40 having descended from the seventy souls who went down into Egypt 237 years before. This statement of time is based on the Septuagint rendering of Ex. xii. 40, which the negative critics assume to be correct. Professor Green says of it: "The gloss thus put upon this passage in Exodus, as it seemed to have the authority of an inspired apostle in its favor in Gal. iii. 17, and as the genealogy of Moses, Ex. vi. 16-20, appeared to preclude the supposition that 430 years were spent in Egypt, became the well-nigh universal view of the case. It still has its advocates, *though the leading Biblical scholars of Europe have abandoned it.*"

On the passage in Galatians, Dr. Green says: "This language of the apostle, however, does not appear to us to be decisive of the point at issue. The interval of time is *only incidentally* mentioned. *Precision of statement regarding it was of no consequence to his argument.*" His opinion upon the chronology itself is very emphatic: "The *evidence is*, we think, *conclusive* that the *abode in Egypt* lasted 430 years. This is the natural sense of Ex. xii. 40, and none would ever think of extracting a different meaning from it, but for reasons outside of the verse itself."

This nobly illustrates a recent deliverance from the same pen upon the untrammeled freedom that should be accorded to the Higher Criticism in discharging its appropriate functions. Even an inspired apostle may be historically inaccurate, when his statement is merely incidental, and precision is of no consequence to his argument. One would suppose that the same principle might apply to the incidental mention by our Saviour, in quoting from the Old Testament, of the name of any author with whose writings the passage adduced was connected by Jewish tradition and in common thought. In every such instance his purpose was to identify it to his hearers as of recognized divine authority. The human authorship was secondary and insignificant, not in the least affecting the purport and power of the words that are cited, whether legal or prophetic.

It is worthy of note that the author's distinguished scholarship would not permit him, in either of the above examples of historical inaccuracy, to refer to a difference in the autograph manuscript, as even possible. Any want of precision in the genealogies was evidently wrought into their original substance. In the Epistle to the Galatians a change in the original reading by a copyist or corrector is precluded by the manifest fact that St. Paul, according to his established custom, followed the Septuagint.

VIII.

MORAL INCONGRUITIES.

The scope of the recent discussions centering upon the alleged inerrancy of the Scriptures was not broad enough to include all that properly belongs to the subject. For this reason it was impossible that by any protraction it should reach a thoroughly satisfactory conclusion.

The only errancy asserted or denied related to empirical matters,—history, science, and the like,—for which men ordinarily depend upon their own observation and the testimony of others. It seemed strange that no one should think of moral errancy in the Bible, as existent, or even possible. Yet it has long been recognized by Christian thought, that there is a contrast between the spirit and teachings of our Saviour, and those of the earlier revelation.

The connection between minor inaccuracies in historical and scientific statement, and imperfect conceptions of right and wrong, as estimated by the highest standard, does not seem to have been discerned. They differ in their nature and kind, yet nothing can be surer than that they are similar in origin, and in the principle upon which their presence in an inspired book must be explained.

They alike indicate that the independent activity of a human agent in the revelation was not so absolutely under the repression and control of the inspiring Spirit as we, in our imperfect wisdom, are apt to think essential to the surest guidance. We must conclude that the failure of the *divine* energy utterly to suppress the *human*, must have had an all-sufficient reason in the import and purpose of the revelation, and this reason it may not be very difficult to find.

The combination that we suggest here is important. For any considerations that will account for the greater and unquestionable errancy, will fully account for the less.

Let us then face fairly these imperfections in the ethical sphere. Objections to the moral lessons of the Old Testament, sometimes as presenting repulsive conceptions of God, in what he seemed to approve or disapprove in the government and conduct of human life, are actively employed, even more than errors in science and history, as effective weapons in the most virulent assaults upon revealed religion.

They are perplexing to many who in spite of them believe in the Lord Jesus Christ with all their heart. There are not a few who accept the Old Testament as containing a divine revelation, who are not able to account for serious moral blemishes in a book like this, and reject many of its statements, considering them absolutely incredible under the rule of the God of truth and grace. Who will not say that this option is better than the rejection of the whole?

Such difficulties, pertaining to the substance of religious belief,—the very centre and heart of revelation,—are harder to deal with than those that relate to its shell and husk. The inspired books are more vulnerable here than at all other points. The boldest scoffer of our times in flaunting "*The Mistakes of Moses*" has declared that there are laws in the Mosaic code that would disgrace any modern statute-book, and his assertion cannot reasonably be disputed. He refers for example to punishments that our later civilization would cry out against as bloody, cruel, and shocking beyond conception. One example adduced is the stoning to death of those who perform labor on the Sabbath,—even of a boy gathering sticks for a fire (Ex. xxxi. 14, 15; Num. xv. 32–36); another, the fearful sentence to be executed upon any one who should entice another to idolatry: "If thy brother, the son of thy mother, or thy daughter, or the wife of thy bosom, or thy friend who is as thine own soul, shall entice thee secretly, saying, 'Let us go and serve other gods,' etc., ... thou shalt surely kill him, thy hand shall be first upon him to put him to death, and afterward the hand of the people; thou shalt stone him with stones till he die" (Deut. xiii. 6–10).

Passing over from legal enactments we find similar use made in the interests of infidelity of the utter extermination by divine command of the inhabitants of Canaanitish cities by the Israelites under Joshua, involving the utter destruction of helpless infancy. For we read again and again with reference to individual cities: "He destroyed them, neither left he any therein to breathe," thus educating to the highest

MORAL INCONGRUITIES. 61

intensity every fierce and savage impulse of which barbarians are capable (Josh. x., xi., xii.).

In this connection the black treachery of Jael comes to mind, violating the sacred laws of hospitality; under promise of protection and safety, alluring the discomfited Sisera to her tent, and in order to dissipate all apprehension, bringing him generous refreshment, and then foully murdering him in his sleep. This is the act that is presently celebrated by Deborah the prophetess, even emphasizing as praiseworthy the lying arts by which she accomplished her purposes:

" He asked water, and she gave him milk;
 She brought forth butter in a lordly dish.
 She put her hand to the nail,
  And her right hand to the workman's hammer;
 And with the hammer she smote Sisera,
  She smote off his head, when she had pierced and stricken through his temples."

Of this woman, and with reference to this act, Deborah, a prophetess, and the judge of Israel, who had predicted, " The LORD shall sell Sisera into the hand of a woman," sang a song of triumph (Jud. v. 24):

" Blessed above women shall Jael the wife of Heber the Kenite be,
Blessed above women in the tent."

In this connection we only yet refer to untruthfulness, endorsed, and even commanded by God, the untruthfulness of his most eminent servants in the performance of their highest official acts. There is an instance of this in the history of Samuel, when sent by God to the house of Jesse in Bethlehem, to anoint David as king over Israel (1 Sam. xvi. 1–6). Samuel expostulating asks, "'How can I go? If Saul hear it, he will kill me.' And the LORD said, Take a heifer, and say, 'I am come to sacrifice to the LORD,' and call Jesse to the sacrifice, and I will show thee what thou shalt do; and thou shalt anoint him whom I name unto thee." It may be said that he offered the sacrifice, and therefore his words were true. But the man must be very dull of apprehension, or anxious at all hazards to maintain that Old Testament revelation embodies the highest ideal of truth and virtue, who can deny that the words were intended to deceive Saul with regard to the object of the prophet's journey. The action is boldly, but appropriately, described in the chapter-heading of the Authorized Version: "*Samuel, sent by God, under pretence of a sacrifice, anoints David.*"

A similar case may be found in the history of the prophet Elisha (2 Kings vi. 18–20). The king of Syria sent a large force to Dothan, where Elisha for the time abode, intending to capture, and probably to destroy him. In answer to his prayer the spies who came to the city to search for him were smitten with blindness. When they approached him "he said to them, 'This is not the way, neither is this the city; follow me, and I will bring you to the man whom ye seek.' And it came to pass, when they were come into Samaria, that Elisha said, 'LORD, open the eyes of these men that they may see.' And the LORD opened their eyes and they saw, and they were in Samaria." So his safety was secured by an artifice. We are not distinctly told that the falsehood uttered was in this instance directly suggested by the inspiring Spirit, but the divine power which was essential to its success, and which might as easily have saved him without the violation of truth, was invoked and granted for its confirmation. It must be confessed, however, that it is all, just as it stands, quite in keeping with the morality of the times, and if the falsehood had been avoided, a very artistic, realistic, and effective story would have been quite spoiled.

Those who contend for the absolute inerrancy of the Bible, vindicating the Old Testament and the New on the same basis, as made up of precisely similar material, and making every word as truly divine and immaculate as if suggested by the mechanical inspiration they disclaim, are not aware how many there are that cannot hold to their theory in the face of such obstacles, how many outside their own safe camp are wandering in darkness, repelled from the glorious grace of the New Testament and a divine Saviour by the incomprehensible and discordant elements they find in the mass of writings through which they must grope, as the only legitimate entrance to the temple of truth. We are surely warranted in seeking to win them back, in correcting what we deem mistaken apprehensions of the revelation of God in the Scriptures.

Let us now take our bearings, in order to ascertain precisely where we are, as the result of what we have supposed an advance movement. We are prepared to find that some will regard it as a retreat before the enemy. But we still claim that on general principles the abandonment of an untenable position is not necessarily a weakening of the defence. It may be most emphatically the opposite.

Have we then, it may be asked, an uncertain Scripture? Can we be satisfied when we feel the ground trembling under our feet? What have we that we can rely upon with implicit confidence in matters pertaining to the great God and ourselves, and to the eternal verities?

If we reply that there is an absolutely trustworthy element in the complex mass, which preponderates over the human and imperfect, it may reasonably be asked, how can the divine be distinguished from the human? We hope to have a better answer by and by than we are yet prepared with, or rather, better than can be appreciated until some other things have been said. We are working our way toward results, but not too precipitately.

It is usually assumed that where such questions arise, reason must decide. Those who "have their senses exercised to discern between good and evil" need not be often perplexed. But this is liable to be exclaimed against, as profanely exalting reason above Scripture. To say that we may go boldly through the Bible, and accept as divine and authoritative only what commends itself to our own individual judgment as worthy of God, will be pronounced no better than the baldest rationalism. It must be granted that it sounds somewhat so. But we shall see by and by. It may be that mitigating circumstances will be discovered, that should modify the severity of the judgment, or even so change the quality of the act as utterly to absolve us from the charge of rationalism.

And what if we shall assert that the divine so permeates the human, or rather, that in the purpose of the inspiring Spirit it so includes it, that they cannot be mechanically separated without the mutilation of the system which it was the purpose of God to produce for the instruction and guidance of men, in the past, if not in the present. Do we not read in another department of divine administration of the growing of tares with the wheat, not to be separated till the harvest? And do we not see something like it in the wondrous scheme of divine providence, evil commingled with the good, the evil suffered and the good directly originated by the divine will, and the evil so often overruled for good, and itself the means of greater good in the future? God will effect the separation in due time. Meanwhile if we, in the use of conscience and enlightened reason, distinguish between them in moral decisions that relate to the regulation of our own lives, shall we be charged with rationalism?

With reference to error other than moral, we may surely claim with abundant warrant in Scripture that this revelation was of such excellent and enduring quality and nature, that its substance and spirit were not bound down to the letter, and could not be injured by great variation from the inspired statement, involving even some inaccuracies in matters of fact. We have already referred to our Saviour's indorsement and free use of a translation which no textual critic would employ in restoring the original readings, except most cautiously and discriminatively; a translation which is often paraphrastic, and in prophecy as well as in history, widely astray from the inspired thought; a translation which pushes forward a hundred years the age of each antediluvian patriarch at the birth of his eldest son, and by its plausible perversion of the Hebrew text in the instance we have mentioned at the close of Chapter VII., betrayed an apostle into chronological inaccuracy. The opinion of Prof. Green as there cited, justifying St. Paul's inaccuracy, is conclusive, and embodies a principle of immense value, as applicable to many similar cases: "*Precision of statement was of no consequence to his argument.*"

We do not, however, desire to ignore or treat with contempt the honest fear of those who are thinking of infidel attack and apologetic controversy, and that if we concede that the Old Testament is not inerrant to the letter everything precious is sacrificed. They fear that all is lost if any one of the alleged "mistakes of Moses" should be proven, or if it be conceded that any prophet, poet, or historian has used language which does not accord with the highest conception of God, or the most perfect results of his grace in the thoughts and lives of men.

But can any one seriously contend that our confidence in the Bible as a genuine revelation must be abandoned, even should we be obliged to admit that the memoir of Adam is a myth, the story of Jonah a drama, or the Book of Daniel the production of a later age than tradition has assigned to it?

Yet let it not be supposed that these interrogative and hypothetical concessions represent the personal opinion of the writer. They only express the strength of his conviction that no conclusions that may be reached with reference to matters so far from the centre of light and truth can shake the hold of these Scriptures upon his heart.

IX.

TURNING FORWARD. — GENERAL CONSIDERATIONS.

EXAMPLES of imperfection in the Scriptures, of the kind indicated in the foregoing chapters, might be multiplied indefinitely. But enough doubtless have been given to arouse in many minds the most serious apprehension—enough to discredit the whole volume, unless a broader definition can be found for the inspiration that produced it than any that has yet been advanced. It may be questioned by some whether a reasonable and intelligible definition can ever be adjusted to phenomena so contrary to prevailing conceptions of the possible contents of an inspired book.

Especially shocking are its moral blemishes. God may *permit* evil to be done without launching his thunderbolts against it. But can he *do* evil, or suggest it, or approve and reward it? And what corrective can be compounded for the injury that may result from such disclosures? To devout readers of the Bible it has been an ideal of perfectness, in accordance with whose rulings all human conduct must be judged, and approved or condemned. What shall they do, if their ideal is shattered before their eyes?

It were better, it may be said, not to have spoken so plainly, and even under sceptical pressure, not to admit so much,—better to have left men the comfort even of a delusion,—than to destroy their confidence in the consummate immaculateness of the Scriptures.

There must indeed have been a shrinking from the task, it would probably have been declined as too painful, if relief from perplexities had not been visible in the distance—reasons why God should employ fallible men as the medium of communication with their kind, and might suffer their work to contain such errors as in his judgment would not impair the ultimate moral purpose and value of the revelation, but might, on the contrary, greatly enhance its effectiveness.

It may not be the way that our poor human sagacity would have indicated, if we had been permitted to suggest the best method. But "the foolishness of God is wiser than men, and the weakness of God is stronger than men." By profounder thought we may discover this, even in imperfections the mention of which is vehemently exclaimed against, as only evil and destructive.

What is inspiration? It is a question of surpassing interest,—one that can no longer be evaded. Even within the few days that have elapsed since the preceding chapters were written it has become evident that the investigations that are to determine the ecclesiastical standing of two distinguished Theological Professors will turn principally upon their denial of the inerrancy of the Bible, as contrary to the cardinal doctrine taught in the Scriptures and in the Confession of Faith of the Presbyterian Church, that "the Scriptures of the Old and New Testaments are the only infallible rule of faith and practice."

Much as religious controversy is to be deplored, if even in the heat of controversy a definition might be forged that shall remove its cause, all will be well. Too often these ardent discussions open up new differences of opinion, excite acrimony, and separate rather than unite. Let our fervent supplications ascend that in this instance an issue so disastrous may be averted.

It was stated in the second chapter that the theory of the absolute inerrancy of Scripture is an *a priori* conclusion. That is, it does not result from observation and thought directed to facts, but is derived inferentially from an antecedent. It is reasoning from cause to effect, determining from the former what we shall find in the latter.

This is an excellent way of attaining some probability, if not certainty, in the absence of known facts. But it is speculative and very fallacious. A conclusion reached by this process should never be affirmed positively unless the antecedent is axiomatic, nor unless furthermore it is sure that no contingency can possibly have occurred that might invalidate the inference. Those not accustomed to the technicalities of logic are not aware of the mental process by which their conviction upon this subject has been reached, if not by themselves, by those from whose teaching they have imbibed it.

In this case the matter to be determined is the absolute perfectness of the Scriptures in every part. The antecedent is inspiration by the Holy Spirit; properly, the inspiration of the prophets or other mediators of a divine revelation; inferentially, of their writings. But the inference is not simple and direct. There are *two* middle terms, either of which may modify the effectiveness of the antecedent, and consequently the soundness of the conclusion. The *first* is that the inspiring Spirit is possessed of perfect knowledge and cannot directly communicate any error. This is unquestionable. The *second* is an inference from the first, namely, that any person or writing inspired by the Spirit must be absolutely inerrant, whatsoever obstruction may intervene. It is included in a more general proposition, that every divine activity must produce absolute perfection, without reference to any contingencies or intermediate conditions. This is most decidedly questionable—to be tested and verified. If any product of creative power can be discovered that was not, at the first moment of its existence, perfect as God is perfect, that despatches it. The *a priori* process, relied upon for proof of the inerrancy of Scripture, is vitiated hopelessly. The premises have failed and the conclusion is a nullity.

We have proposed to reverse the process. The results of inspiring energy are before us in a divine revelation. We all agree upon that. All theories and hypotheses are to be tested by facts, if facts are within reach. The revelation, as expressed by human language and thought in the Scriptures, exhibits the *phe-*

INSPIRATION.

nomena of inspiration. By their careful examination we may get some glimpse of the *noumena*, or divine conceptions in which they originate. In other words, we may learn from the study of the Scriptures something about the inspiration that produced them, and how far it has been deflected from its proper ideal perfectness by earthly conditions.

We shall then be prepared to produce a definition *a posteriori*, reasoning from the effect to its cause, from the consequent to the antecedent, from the revelation that lies before us in the Bible to the principle and method of the originating divine activity.

If we discover errors of fact, or any imperfections, we shall learn by the same careful induction how and why they have obtained entrance; and also how unimportant they are, in any sense that depreciates the value of the Book,—and how important and valuable, if not necessary, was the divine sufferance of these blemishes in the accomplishment of the ruling purpose of the revelation.

It scarcely needs to be said that the Bible does not define inspiration. Neither does it contain any statement upon the subject that implies the absolute perfectness of what was spoken or written by the bearer of a divine revelation. The reference to Scripture as "*God-inspired*" in 2 Tim. iii. 16 does not, nor the reference to holy men of God as "*moved by the Holy Ghost*," in 1 Pet. i. 21. Neither of these expressions intimates the degree in which the prophet's mental activities were controlled by the inspiring Spirit. It is nowhere asserted that those who are inspired thereby become possessed of all knowledge, nor that they are elevated morally and intellectually above all possibility of mistake or error, so that the thought of man can never in the future, even by divine aid, attain better results.

The contrary is implied in 1 Cor. xiii. 9–12, where St. Paul says of apostolic utterances in general, "For we know *in part*, and we prophesy *in part*"; "now we see through a glass darkly"; and he compares his own present inspiration, in its contrast to the perfect disclosures of the future, to the difference in thought and speech between childhood and mature age. If error were impossible under the divine afflatus we should not find the martyr Stephen, when "full of the Holy Ghost," and his face transformed through the inspiration "as it had been the face of an angel," making unconsciously at least two statements that contradict the Old Testament (Acts vii., viii.). Even the convenient evasion that these errors may have resulted from the carelessness of copyists has never been ventured here.

Especially, if inspiration implies inerrancy, it could not have been possible that one apostle should say of another, who was acting under the highest official responsibility as the leader and guide of a body of Christians, "I withstood him to the face because he was to be blamed" (Gal. iii. 12). But with the consciousness that they are not perfect, the prophets and apostles exhibit a firm conviction that they are bearers of a divine and authoritative message, and they sometimes distinguish their inspired instructions from the products of their own thought.

It was intimated at the beginning that the task of framing a fresh definition of the inspiration of the Scriptures in place of that which thorough Biblical discipline finds untenable, is very difficult. We are sufficiently warned against other *a priori* definitions, not ascertained by thorough induction. An early college recollection has not died out, of a conceited Sophomore who amused his companions, upon hearing them compare notes about the respective amounts of their reading in history, by scornfully declaring his own superior method: "I lay down my principles, and deduce my facts." A delightful labor-saving way of attaining certain knowledge, with the advantage of being able to deposit in one's repertory just what facts may seem desirable. This would be all very well for a dream-world,—if one might weave airy fancies and without contact with his fellow-men ascend straightway to heaven. But this hard world declines to accept such facts, and asks sharp questions testing their validity.

The theory of verbal inspiration is compact and simple,—apparently a short and easy method of repelling the assaults of scepticism. The claim that the Bible is all—every word and syllable—the product of divine suggestion, seems to be one that must silence all questioning,—that is, if it can be successfully maintained against the keen scrutiny of hostile criticism.

But not unfrequently the very simplicity and convenience of a proposed method of performing work or escaping difficulty, is suspicious. This is especially so where the conditions to be provided for are complex and variable, as they surely are in the subject before us. In a definition, obscurity and inadequacy may result from a desire to use terms that are general and comprehensive, that exhibit, it may be, a mere abstraction, supposed to be applicable to innumerable special instances, with the consequent merit of conciseness, and apparent freedom from all possibility of entanglement. But when we come to distribute the general into the particulars it is supposed to cover or contain, these may be found to differ so widely in character and quality as to pass beyond the limit it was thought would include them.

This is so to a remarkable degree with our present theme. The component elements in the revelation are so varied in substance and in form, in time and in conditions, and the issue is so complicated by the presence of a human coefficient, that a satisfactory definition of the divine energy involved in the joint product, cannot be compressed into a single sentence.

Inspiration, considered merely as a word, may be sufficiently defined after the fashion of our dictionaries by the equivalent and simpler word *in-breathing*. But this leaves us as far as ever from any clear conception of the act. Or if, after the *a priori* method we have described, we begin with the highest conception of the truth and power of God, and the consequent necessary perfection of his work, as our postulate, and claim inferentially that the breathing of his Holy Spirit into the minds of men must produce the absolute exactness of every word spoken or written under that influence, our conclusion may possibly seem to us, in the insufficiency of our training in dialectics, to be fully warranted by the severest logic. But we may be called to face and account for many instances in which some counter influence has impaired the perfect expression of the divine thought and will, and our definition has made no provision against such failure. We stand aghast, and are helpless. We can only vociferate against the irreverence that refuses our definitions, quote irrelevantly from Scripture or incoherently from Confessions, and if possible, stamp out the heresy by ecclesiastical arraignment. But it is all in vain. Facts are stubborn. Galileo may be scorched by the inquisition, *but the earth revolves.*

It will be understood as beyond question that no human intelligence can penetrate the mystery pertaining to the interior relation and combined efficiency of the two incomprehensible factors. Our Saviour's wonderful comparison of the work of the Spirit in the new birth to the wind, will apply to inspiration as well as to regeneration. Yet by moving slowly we may get a sufficient idea for all practical purposes. Here, as often in the presence of the Infinite, we must needs skim the surface. But an explanation confined to the indisputable phenomena in the documents which we hold as inspired, will meet all the requirements of the case as connected with our present embarrassment.

It must be kept steadily before us, that not from a preconception, but *a posteriori*, from the character and design of the revelation as now to be developed, and in connection with all that it necessarily implies, we are to obtain a suitable idea of the agency that produced it. It may be that in order to this, our conception of both these important words needs broadening.

X.

INSPIRATION DEFINED BY REVELATION.

The Bible in its unity may be correctly described as a revelation. This is a compact statement, apparently very simple and intelligible. But the word *revelation*, like *inspiration*, is somewhat ambiguous and indeterminate. In order to be of service in solving our problem it needs to be defined.

Yet it is a very graphic word. Even upon its surface it is splendidly illuminative in describing the substance and significance of the Bible in its entire breadth, history and doctrine, prophecy and poetry. Strictly speaking, inspiration is only concerned in publishing a revelation to those for whom it was intended, in such method and form as shall best insure its efficiency with reference to some divine purpose. We see at once that while the two differ, they are nearly related, and our knowledge of one must aid us in acquiring a knowledge of the other.

The word *revelation* is usually limited to utterances that embody truth or fact not before known, and which might never have become known except through special illumination. If this were all, it would not apply to a very large part of the Bible,—to many historical Books scarcely at all. But the limitation cannot be maintained.

DEFINED BY REVELATION. 79

We have already seen that all Scripture—historic, prophetic, and didactic—is material for Biblical Theology. It has become evident that new aspects of divine power, wisdom, holiness, justice, truth, and grace, as interwoven from the first with human affairs, may be disclosed in accounts that contain nothing supernatural in the ordinary sense of the term, but are made up of events that have been ascertained through personal observation of the historian, or information by others. The transcendent value of the revelation lies rather in its containing sublime facts concerning God's dealings with men, than in the record that details them, or the inspiration by which it was produced.

We ask, then, as a preliminary inquiry, *What is revelation?* Its helpfulness will appear almost immediately.

It is one of the figurative words from the Latin that enrich our language. It precisely corresponds with *apocalypse* from the Greek, whose related verb is always in the New Testament translated *reveal*. Literally it denotes a divine activity in *putting aside a veil*, in order that something may be seen which was before invisible. The noun is often used passively of that which is revealed or disclosed, as in the title to the last Book in the Bible, *The Revelation of St. John*.

The word itself is of less consequence to our present purpose than *its necessary implications*. It implies a divine activity, and a definite purpose in its exercise. It also implies a subject-matter to be revealed, and a recipient. The *subject*, the *recipient*, and *the divine purpose* particularly concern us now, and must be successively treated in their bearing upon the principal inquiry: *What is revealed? To whom is it revealed?* and *with what design?* The replies to these questions, in their present significance for our purpose, lie close together.

Is it possible to answer the first of these questions comprehensively in a single word? What is revealed? What substance underlies the phenomena of the revelation? Surely the Bible throughout its whole extent reveals *God—the one living God*.

Yet not his existence in the abstract, as a matter of philosophic thought; but in his voluntary relations with men, as a wise, righteous, and almighty moral Governor, a loving Father, and a gracious Saviour—in all admirable, attractive, and endearing qualities.

Here two of the implications in the word, combine. The Revealer is also himself the revelation. No attribute of his nature is more strongly marked than that which is described by the adjective *self-revealing*. He is always manifesting himself in aspects important to men. This was the light shining in darkness from the beginning. Every divine name is the revelation of some sublime truth concerning God, to be known and cherished as of the deepest interest to those who are involved in the misery of sin. Every providential activity exhibits him as a God near, and not afar off, to be feared, to be obeyed, to be trusted, to be sought in every time of trouble.

In this revelation everything is brought down to

the simplest narrative form, so that even children may apprehend it. There are no metaphysical abstractions. Here are impressive stories of individual life in great variety—of men, women, and children in circumstances of special interest, appealing to the heart of the great Father, and not in vain—and the history of families and nations, severally, and in their commingling and contests.

These graphic delineations are the external investiture in which the God of heaven and earth presents himself before the eyes of men, and he is the living spirit within. It is a grand panorama of ever shifting scenes, broken up, fragmentary, in successive and varied glimpses, here a little and there a little. The material is diversified and the transitions are frequent, but therefore all the more effective. All that men could bear, and more than they could understand all at once, are simply and visibly portrayed in this revelation.

Its chief characteristics are motion and life—God's life as the "fountain of life," in association with man's life in all its minute details, ever bearing on, in the majesty of power, the beauty of holiness, and the glory of infinite righteousness and grace—ever bearing on toward the restoration of all things.

The subject-matter of the revelation, then, is God, an infinite nature, as coming into intimate relations with men in their moral darkness and degradation, dissipating the darkness by the holy light of his love and truth, and lifting the fallen into the highest honor and blessing in fellowship with himself.

The revelation in the first instance was to the prophet, as the divinely appointed spokesman for God. He must express in human language the divine conception with which he was inspired, as nearly as he could. There could never be more than an approximation. He might possibly have expressed it in variant forms, none of them fully including or representing, yet none of them dishonoring, its inexhaustible comprehensiveness.

But an important distinction must be made here. When we speak of a communication concerning God addressed to the ears or eyes of men, as a revelation, it was not a revelation to them, in the same sense that the underlying thought was a revelation to the prophet, but only in a poor, objective, and superficial way. It only embodied, as well as the limitations of human thought and the poverty of human speech would permit, revealable truth. For all true revelation is subjective, interior. It is the voice of God, not speaking from a distance—far away in the heavens, no one knows where—but vibrating in one's inmost soul, in tones which he hears and in language he understands. The God who lives in the system of nature, and expresses in its laws his thought and will, dwells much more in men, the life of their life, and the centre and support of their being. He reveals himself to them as *immanent*—a word that distinguishes the true, practical, and precious philosophy of religion, which we cannot expand now, but shall say more of in its place—ever working from within and not from without—in nature and much more in

DEFINED BY REVELATION. 83

man, producing slowly but surely all beautiful results—God immanent, to be glorified forever.

A true and actual revelation of God implies as its indispensable co-ordinate, apprehension. It describes a process that is only complete when the truth disclosed, through the quickening grace of the Spirit, reaches the mind and heart. A hidden revelation is a contradiction in terms. A candle put under a bushel is not an illumination. For the present, however, we use the word in its current sense, as outward and not inward. There will be occasion for something further in considering the recipients of the revelation.

With this preamble as the first step in inquiring for the subject-matter of the revelation, we turn to the Bible in its scope, plan, and the relation of its principal parts as exhibited in Biblical Theology. For we have the advantage of having its substance and contents thoroughly prepared by capable and conscientious scholarship for our inductive consideration.

The first thing that impresses us in the general aspect of the Bible, is that it is composed of many portions, and these in succession of time, sweeping over the whole period of man's existence upon the earth, down to the revelation of the Son of God incarnate as the glorious finality.

Even the first of these portions, the Book of Genesis, the book of the beginning and origin of all things, is manifold. It contains every record possessed by the Jewish nation of God's relations with men, and every communication from God for many centuries; and it relates to great varieties of condition and need.

This is very important in our search, as characteristic of the whole. We have in the Bible, not one comprehensive revelation of God to all men and for all time, general in its nature and uniform in texture and scope. But many successive revelations are here, often with wide space between, each having its own specific character, and adapted to the exigency of some special time.

The purpose, significance, and value of some of these communications were nearly or quite exhausted very soon after they were made. There may be some general principle of permanent value, underlying any special revelation. But that principle may have been well known before, or it may be axiomatic, and sure to be repeated in subsequent disclosures. But the precise conditions to which its form was adapted can never be renewed.

We infer confidently that no theory or definition of inspiration is adequate that treats it as uniform in the measure and value of its results, and equally good for all time and in all connections.

No definition is adequate that fails to recognize the historical and progressive principle in this revelation, or to distinguish between the meagreness and imperfection of its earlier stages, which only partly displaced the crudeness and narrowness of human thought, and the divine fulness and perfection of the final revelation of grace and truth in Jesus Christ; as well as all intermediate gradations, each of the long series, in general, rising to a somewhat higher level than that which preceded it.

St. Paul made this distinction, referring to the Old Testament as a whole, especially as symbolized by the theophany upon Sinai, and the temporary illumination of Moses' face when he came down out of the Mount: "For if that which passeth away is with glory, much more shall that which remaineth be in glory" (2 Cor. iii. 2. R. V.)

Let the above suggestion be borne in mind, as a valuable contribution to the *a posteriori* definition we are in quest of. Historical progression, implying earlier insufficiency, is a leading characteristic of the divine method of inspiration.

XI.

THE HUMAN COEFFICIENT IN REVELATION.

IF the self-revelation of God in the Scriptures had been accomplished by immediate and independent activity, or if the human agency employed had been passive and mechanical, the subject of inspiration would have been far less difficult.

But it originates in the activity of two personal factors, whose respective products are not so easily distinguishable as might be imagined, considering how much they differ. They are combined in the same fabric, and so intimately that separation is impossible. Yet we know that in individual contrast divine thought is higher than human thought as the heavens are higher than the earth.

This is a "mystical union" not mentioned as such in our theologies. It is just here that our feeble comprehension is most thoroughly baffled. We can know either factor alone only in part,—the life and Spirit of God, or the life and spirit of man. In these Scriptures they blend, the higher infusing itself into the lower for gracious purposes, and with wondrous adaptation of means to the end.

These inspired compositions throughout bear the

human impress and stamp, and that of various human individuality. This is partly exhibited in differences of style. It lies in the use of severally characteristic forms of words and structure of sentences,—in the more or less elevated, ornate, or impassioned utterance of thought,—in comparative clearness or obscurity of expression,—in differences of tone that indicate difference in temperament,—in a varying experience as affecting the feelings and character—strains pitched upon the major key of exhilaration and hope predominating in one, and those upon the minor key of depression and discouragement in another.

It is noteworthy here that this human coloring, taking its precise shade from the individual agency employed, is even more strongly marked in prophecy, with its oft-recurring formula, "Thus saith the Lord," —as if every word were purely divine,—than in history, professedly written by men. This would seem to indicate that the great God not only condescended to use the language of men in some general way, but, whenever he employs men as his messengers, must needs transform himself into an Isaiah, a Jeremiah, or an Ezekiel, as respects all individual characteristics of feeling and expression, having no style of his own. Something of the same kind has been observed, and commented upon unintelligently by hostile criticism, in the resemblance between the diction and style of the Apostle John, and that of our Saviour in the discourses recorded in the last of the Gospels.

The Scriptural idea of inspiration, then, even in its higher flights, admits of the divine thought being cast into any human mould that may be selected, and bearing its impress so completely that one judging by the exterior form might pronounce it thoroughly human, yet claiming to be so divine as to be introduced by a "*Thus saith the* Lord."

If we turn to the historical Books, it might seem to superficial thought that only human observation, sagacity, and faithfulness were required, or, if inspiration is implied at all, that its office was little less than absolutely passive, nearly a sinecure. The earlier treatises on inspiration make a distinction between the inspiration of suggestion, and that of mere superintendence; the latter finding its place in historic detail, its province confined to guarding against accidental oversight. If the agents were thoroughly qualified long histories might have been prepared without need of the active aid or interference of the superior power.

This might be true of these histories, if correctness were the only requisite to the fulfillment of the divine purpose in their preparation.

But remembering what they contain, in its highest significance and value—the story of God's gracious achievements, guidance, and general providential activity in directing all human affairs; remembering what was stated in describing Biblical Theology, that there is a revelation of the living God in the facts here recorded, no less than in didactic or prophetic utterances, and that these must be related, if they are to be effective for good, not as dry-as-dust chronicles, principally of value to the professional antiquarian or historian, but in such a way as to make an impression upon the hearts of all readers, in such a way that the wisdom of God in providential appointments and deliverances may be duly appreciated,—remembering all this, how necessary it is that all the higher faculties of the narrator should be so wrought upon as to do their very best work, every human power that might contribute to its completeness and effectiveness aroused to its highest capacity by the divine Spirit, who penetrates the deepest recesses of the heart, and turns it whithersoever he will.

It is to this that we are indebted for the charm of many of the beautiful and impressive Old Testament stories. It is owing to this that our children never become weary of hearing them, and their lessons of faith, obedience, and courage, on the part of men, and of wisdom, power, love, and truth, in God, sink into the depths of their hearts and can never be forgotten.

They find here exquisite tales of the personal relations of men in weakness, sore peril, and distress, with the great God who rules in omnipotence in the heavens and in the earth—tales of his tender care and sympathy with their sufferings and dangers.

They read of little Samuel responding to the call of God as he lay by night on his tiny couch in the temple—of the lad Joseph imprisoned in a cave, and sold by his heartless brothers to Ishmaelites of the desert—of baby Moses wailing in the bulrushes—of Daniel in the lion's den, and of a score of others.

A mother's lips may translate them into language suited to the age of her eager listeners. Her version may not be exact to the letter. But do not rebuke her inaccuracies, as if verbal precision were all-important. She and their heavenly Father know them better than we—what will fix their attention—and what they can bear. The inspiring Spirit could scarcely improve upon the inspiration of a mother's heart, or at least, he condescends to use it for his own gracious purpose. There is no danger of her spoiling the story, or marring its effect, by her apparent perversion. The blessed substance is there, and may be exhibited with many delicate and delightful departures and interludes, like the variations of a skillful composer upon some of our dear old tunes, each adding a fresh charm to the original melody.

Here we see what gave their prevailing historic form to these early products of inspiration. They are addressed through the intellect to a part of the nature more susceptible to impression, and influential over the life, especially in those not trained to abstract thought, who constitute the great bulk of mankind. They cannot understand a philosophy, however simply it may be stated and explained. But exhibit it dramatically in the incidents of personal life, and they follow you with the deepest interest; not an item is lost. They drink it in eagerly and its moral impressions abide. Here lies the power of graphic narrative, depicting stirring scenes in individual existence, of prophetic utterances as woven into the history of men, and of inspired personal prayer and communion with God, in connection with personal danger and deliverance.

Thus even human history may be luminous with divine wisdom, truth, and love. Perchance poor, silly men may be convinced by such lessons that the everlasting God will become their friend, if they crave his friendship. If they call in their hour of need, he will hear them as he heard others before them. These lessons come to them most effectively through men of like passions with themselves, human hearts and human lips relating a personal experience of the mercy and faithfulness of God.

It might be feared, however, that any advantage in moral impression through the employment of men as mediators of the revelation, might be more than counterbalanced by resulting impairment, that the glorious light of divine revelation would surely be darkened through the imperfect transmission of its rays. Let us have, it might be said, God's own precise words, without human intellection intervening. Then we shall know that we have truth, and nothing but the exact truth.

This is very plausible, but God knows better than we. Our *a priori* judgment is a delusion, and in conflict with fact. What if it be granted as fairly proven that some slight impairment in the exterior form has occurred, and that this was permitted by God, and wrought into his plan as thereby more effective for his purpose?

Here Biblical Theology advances to our aid, with its careful scrutiny, in accordance with its principle and methods as already described. It takes the Scriptures apart, and carefully observing the historic order, so far as it can be approximately ascertained by the preliminary discipline, it judges each principal portion, both in general scope and in detail, by its own specific period and its manifest purpose as then to be accomplished, and not by the advanced illumination and needs of our own more favored time. It enables us to understand how a genuine revelation of God may be somewhat impaired, its images confused, discolored and distorted, by passing through an imperfect medium, not transparent, but feebly translucent; yet the impairment graciously permitted, because the divine thought was thus better adapted to the still lower intellectual and spiritual apprehension it was intended to reach.

The prophet is a man, not over-wise, and only partially receptive to divine truth; and the people to whom he is sent are human, and much more ignorant than he. The Deity as discerned through this narrow human capacity, the higher as well as the lower, the prophet and the people alike, is necessarily in some degree humanized, anthropomorphic, brought down to man's native standard of thought, feeling, and action. The objective illumination was perfect. The prophet took in for the people what he could, and could give them no more than he had. As an exhibition of the God of glory, it was poor, feeble, and unworthy. Nevertheless, it was much nearer the true conception, than could have been possible, but for the revelation.

Through the inspiration came light, at first glimmering faintly through the darkness; yet true light, for darkness cannot emit even the faintest glimmer. It is like the omnipotent touching of the blind man's eyes, as related in the Gospels. He saw very obscurely, but he actually *saw*. His vision was far from perfect at first. It was very poor. The objects before it were uncertain in outline, color, and movement, and blurred in all minor details. But notwithstanding, it was true vision, and not optical illusion. It conveyed some correct apprehension to the brain. It was *men* that were seen, not grotesque monsters; as *trees*, not as reptiles prone to the earth; *walking*, not crawling.

So in the Old Testament. The divine impress is upon it all. It is the light shining in darkness,—not our midday sunlight, but relatively bright and pure, suggesting unlimited possibilities of increase,—cast athwart the opacity and moral abomination of heathendom. Even that degraded heathendom must receive from it some glimpse of a higher type of divinity than it had ever before recognized—a living God, a spiritual God, a personal God, a holy God; one that can see, hear, speak, promise, threaten, reward, punish, projecting himself into the life and history of men, so far as they were capable of apprehending him.

He comes in the person of his accredited messenger into the presence of a high earthly mightiness,— one that had never trembled at the presence of man, that knows no loftier worship than that of birds, and beasts, and creeping things, or of the lifeless forces of nature. It is the great Jehovah who speaks, but through human lips, and in terms adapted to human thought: "Israel is my son, even my first-born, and I have said unto thee, 'Let my son go that he may serve me,' and thou hast refused to let him go. Behold, I will slay thy son, even thy first-born." The God that so speaks is no *scarabaeus* of Egyptian mythology, and the human consciousness of such times could not have originated him. The message bears his impress and superscription—divine upon its face—and Pharaoh quails before it, and yields to a power greater than his own.

In some way—we need not know how—God thrusts forth into our murky atmosphere a pure thought concerning himself, to be caught up and apprehended by human faculties according to their condition and capacity. The form which it exhibits on these historic pages is principally the result of human brainwork, the best possible at the time. The delineation is full of life and power, but to the highest intelligence, as educated by later revelation, while often charming and most attractive, it is sometimes repellent, or even utterly intolerable.

Is it possible to find relief in the preceding paragraph from the thought of the atrocities practised in taking possession of Canaan, as referred to in a former chapter? All the inhabitants of many populous cities were ruthlessly slain, and it is stated that God commanded their utter extermination. Imagine Joshua with the armies of Israel under his control, charged with an imperative divine commission to put an end to the idolatry of the land throughout all its borders, and to the shameful practices that defiled it as in the days of Sodom. The commission may not have been in words, but in an impulse which he recognized by infallible signs as not emanating from his own will, but from the will of God. Inspired by the most exalted zeal for the honor of Jehovah, but with sensibilities deadened by the cruel usages of the warfare of his time, may he not have felt himself authorized and impelled by the Holy Spirit to consume the accursed race, root and branch? Confusing his own savage instincts with the promptings of the true inspiration within him, he asserted with perfect sincerity a divine warrant and command.

It is a conjecture and cannot be verified. But it may lie upon the borders of possible deliverance from the oppression we feel when we read in the Bible descriptions so contrary to the teachings of our Saviour,—that an impulse in its origin divine and holy may undergo a fearful change in its transition to consummated acts. The meteorolite, a fragment detached from a much larger mass in its revolution around the sun, moves with inconceivable swiftness and cleaves ether or space, invisible and noiseless. But coming within the sphere of the earth's attraction and atmosphere, it burns with fierce heat, and bursts asunder with terrific force, and with destruction to everything in its way. So a pure and righteous emotion of hatred to moral perversity breathed into the heart of a man may become fierce, cruel, and implacable.

We need not be disturbed if we do not find in the earliest inspiration the spirit and the deeds that we enjoy in this later time, as walking in the light of divine love incarnate in our Saviour, with the advantage it gives us in all right conception of things human and divine. If we should be transported from our present illumination into that past, having what God gave to the men of the time, and no more, the contrast would overwhelm us, and we should be of all men the most miserable.

But again, let us not be disturbed. Whatsoever we have through divine grace, we shall have and hold forever, with as much more as the God of revelation will give us. There is no retrograde evolution to be apprehended, no going back from the advanced day-dawn to the midnight shimmer of the stars,—much less to the primeval darkness of the chaotic world.

No, surely not, with a single proviso,—unless in moral perversity we make choice of the evil. There is a sad power in will, even in our poor human will—a power of retrocession, of shutting off from our vision what we do not wish to behold.

But barring that, we are all right, and on the ascending grade,—from faith to faith, from strength to strength, from light to light, from life to life, from glory to glory, even as by the Spirit of the Lord.

XII.

REVELATION KEEPING PACE WITH DEVELOPMENT.

WHILE we are yet thinking of God as revealing himself to men, we must not leave unconsidered the co-ordinate and proportional advance, as in living unison, of the principle and its product, of the cause and the effect. The divine manifestation and the human apprehension move forward together toward a goal in the future,—the perfected Christ of the Gospels, reproduced in the lives of men.

By a persistence of the original energy a historic revelation increases in clearness and efficiency, and this with distinct reference to the growth of its recipients in knowledge and grace, growth ever stimulating growth.

How like this is to the advance, from stage to stage, and from form to form, in the sphere of nature since the first creative act! What name shall we give to the principle or law that connects all phenomena, spiritual and physical, with other preceding phenomena in which they apparently, and in some respects really, originate,—although not by any causation that operates independently of the immediate, immanent presence and pressure of the divine will? Thus carefully guarded, there is no better term than that which modern science has chosen, and might have caught up from the creative account in Genesis, with its *births* or *generations* of successive typical forms, as expressed by a familiar Hebrew word, which always implies *parentage*. The term *evolution*, although less graphic than the Hebrew conception *birth*, describes admirably the principle manifested, not only in the material universe, but in God's self-revelation, in all that addresses itself to the mind, as including all intellective and reasoning faculties, in the *natural* sphere; and also to the heart, the conscience, the will, the affections, and all organs of a highly spiritual nature, in the *moral* sphere.

The writer of these pages is a believer, and ever more intelligently and thoroughly a believer, in a divine principle of evolution. He sees it in the wide and varied outspread of nature, and in all the activities of natural law. For what is natural law, but the human conception of divine and orderly action? He sees it, not only in the rocks, with their fossil remains of vegetable and animal life, but in language, in history, in science, in religion—in things in the heavens and things in the earth—above, beneath, around, everywhere—and so, with the rest, in the revelation of God in the Bible.

It is Herbert Spencer's idea—a magnificent generalization. As expressed by the philosopher it is lamentably deficient, in failing to recognize distinctly the omnipotent, personal God immanent in nature, as its animating and impelling energy. With this indispensable correction, we accept it in principle, with whatever variation in details.

The living personal God is the centre and source of all life, of all organic development, of all advance to more perfect modes of existence, processes, and functions. Nothing is out of his reach and grasp, nothing too great or too insignificant for the exercise of his power. The infinite Spirit in his wise and loving activities is behind the scene. He that was, and is, and shall be—ὅ ἐρχόμενος, *the coming one*—is ever coming out more manifestly from the depths of his infinite nature, infusing himself into, and impressing himself upon, everything that through his will exists. He ever progressively and more distinctly unfolds himself before those who have eyes to see; and so is ever educating their eyes to see more clearly whatever, as his scheme develops, he may yet have to show them.

In this moving, changeful exposition, the grand panorama of all that may be known among men, God, working from within outwardly, is the Exhibitor, wisely adapting the exposition in its breadth and contents to the ever-growing capacity to which it is addressed. Man, the spectator, as well as, in his generations, a principal component in the exhibition, ever beholding more appreciatively, and becoming more deeply interested in the unceasing progression, onward and still onward.

As a consequence, through an inner divine impetus and illumination—this is psychical evolution, one grade higher in the divine process—he invents new appliances, instruments, scientific formulæ, and indescribable methods for observing more accurately, more profoundly, deeper down, farther away in time and space, in the past and in the future. He harnesses in universal nature to bear triumphantly forward the royal chariot of knowledge and truth.

Here come in steam, electricity, and what not,—new discoveries or developments of natural law. All elements and forces are utilized progressively and expansively in subservience to the growth of humanity in wisdom.

Thus all human capacities,—although many of the most efficient workers have not the slightest glimmering of it, perhaps professedly and boastfully agnostic,— are evolving, illustrating, and so magnifying and glorifying God more perfectly. They will understand better hereafter the magnificent proportions and significance of the work in which they have been engaged. Everything in its time.

It is a pleasant thought that many an atheist is a theist in embryo. He calls himself an evolutionist and agnostic. Earnestly studying the great volume of nature,—and most intelligently in his chosen sphere, even if blindly as respects what is above him,—he is working toward the light. He will discover the grand secret by and by, an evolutionist still, but an agnostic no longer.

Yet even a thoughtful child, as he beholds how the world is moving on, may give glory to God. There go the ships, packets and clippers of beautiful mould, flying upon the wings of the wind, coming like a cloud, and like doves to their lattices, from Tarsus and the isles afar off. Then, the steamers; first, for the river, bringing the products of toil from villages and farms to some seaport; next, for the great ocean, moving swiftly and majestically with their enormous contents, distributing people and wealth in every part of the globe. Then, we have railways spanning broad continents, with telegraphs, telephones, electric illumination and electric motors, inventions of every sort; immeasurable capacity, ever pushing forward, forward—who can realize what triumphs may be celebrated at the same rate of advance within the next little century, though but a tiny fragment of the vast eternity beyond?

We shall speak more of this further on, in its bearing upon revelation. We only care now to confirm the principle already asserted, that every divine activity connected with men and their advancement in wisdom and righteousness, and their attainment of ultimate blessedness in completed fellowship with God, is necessarily progressive.

We shall delight in the opportunity, and it will come in due time, of saying something about the personality of God, which modern philosophy denies, as necessarily limiting an infinite nature, and therefore an impossible conception; and on the further question, how far evolution in the domain of spirit, reason, and will, as the substances upon which it operates, corresponds with physical evolution, and how far we may claim for it in the relations of Spirit with spirit, of Mind with mind, of Person with person, and of Will with will—the Infinite with the finite—a higher and freer activity than that of natural law in a material system, with special divine adaptations to changeful moral conditions and needs.

It may appear that the accomplished agnostic, whether scientist, philosopher, or both, is true to his name—that he does not know *all* about the world of thought to which we are led by questions like these. Let him not philosophize here. By his own definition his sphere of knowledge is limited to conditions infinitely lower. "*Ne sutor ultra crepidam.*"

XIII.

THE REVELATION AS ADDRESSED TO MEN.

In the order of thought suggested in the ninth chapter, we are next to consider the nature and needs of those to whom the revelation is addressed, as partially determinative of its principal characteristics.

A flood of light may be thrown upon the inspiration that has given us such a Bible as we have, in its marvellous adaptation to specific ends, if we inquire whether there is anything in men, whether latent or developed, that is appreciatively responsive to this divine condescension, or capable of becoming so. Otherwise, it is casting pearls before swine.

The question is not sufficiently answered by a reference to intelligence and reason. For these faculties, exalted as they are, cannot apprehend the higher realities exhibited in this Holy Book, except under a broader definition than is usually attached to them. With whatever undeveloped capacity for such knowledge our nature was originally endowed, it is now dormant and inoperative.

What if we put together several sentences from the New Testament that bear upon the question. Take one from our Saviour's Sermon on the Mount: "If thine eye be evil, thy whole body shall be full of darkness; if then the light that is in thee be darkness, how great is that darkness." Another is from the Gospel of John: "In him was life, and the life was the light of men. And the light shineth in darkness, and the darkness comprehendeth it not." A third is from the pen of the apostle to the Gentiles: "For the natural (Gr. *psychical*) man receiveth not the things of the Spirit of God, neither can he know them, because they are spiritually (Gr. *pneumatically*, *i.e.*, through the *pneuma*) discerned."

Lest it should seem to some readers that these citations are misconceived in the interests of a too rigid orthodoxy, something may be added from the unorthodox pen of a leading English Unitarian. He has recently been branded a rationalist. But surely in the following language he assigns the right place to the intellect, the pure reason, apart from the moral sensibilities. It would be impossible to make selections more satisfactory from the most orthodox theologian: "The intellect alone, like the telescope waiting for an observer, is quite blind to the celestial things above it,—a dead mechanism dipped in night,—ready to serve as the dioptric glass, spreading the images of light from the Infinite upon the tender and living retina of the conscience." *

Every word of this further quotation should be carefully noted. It occurs just after the above: "In the conscience and moral affections we have our

---

* Prof. James Martineau's "Studies of Christianity," p. 187.

only revealers of God. Let it be understood that I mean, our only *internal* revealers of him; the only faculty of our being capable of furnishing us with the idea and belief of him, with any perception of his character, and allegiance to his will. We mean to state that without this faculty, the bare intellect, the mere scientific and reasoning power, could make no way toward the knowledge of divine realities, could never, by any system of helps whatsoever, be trained or guided into this knowledge, any more than in the absence of the proper sense the *ear* of the blind could be taught *to see;* and that nature, life, history, miracle, notwithstanding their most sedulous discipline, would leave us utterly in the dark about religion, except as they addressed themselves to our consciousness of what is holy, just, beautiful, and great.

"But we do *not* mean that the moral sense can stand alone, dispense with all outward instruction, and supply a man with a natural religion ready made. Nor do we mean that the every-day experience, and the ordinary providence of God, are enough, without special revelation, to lead us to heavenly truth.

"And we are therefore prepared to advance another step, and to say, that while we regard conscience as the only *inward* revealer, we have *faith in Christ*, as *his perfect and transcendent outward revelation.*"

Let these last words be especially remarked. This so-called rationalist leads us directly to the historic Christ—the Christ of the Gospels—as the ultimate source of authority in religion. He exalts him as supreme Lord over every divinely imparted faculty in our nature, the moral and spiritual, as well as the simply intellectual, however perfect their development and culture. He makes him the illuminator of conscience, without whose revelation of God its light is comparatively darkness.

Martineau is the most metaphysical of religionists. His metaphysics have controlled his modes of thought and tinctured his theology. This appears in his denial of the proper Deity of Christ, and at many other points. This is a great pity, but not personally fatal. Disordered metaphysics are deplorable, but will not exclude him from the kingdom of heaven. For in his heart of hearts he adores Christ as "*the most perfect and transcendent outward revelation of God,*" and the voice of Christ, as it addresses him from the written revelation of the Bible, commands his deepest homage as the voice of God, the supreme authority to which every faculty of his nature lovingly and trustfully submits.

It is evident from the preceding extracts that Professor Martineau's psychology corresponds with that of the Bible. Its facts are of immense importance in our search. It is enough for the present that this psychology recognizes in man, not only a rational, intellective principle, called *soul*, but a *spirit* nature of higher function and capacities, able to hold converse with God.

The presence of these elements in his being is recognized in the Biblical account of the creation, especially in his inspiration by the divine breath, which distinguished Adam from other living creatures upon the earth. Yet it is easy to fall into the error of attributing high perfection to the divine principle that exalted him, and consequently a higher intelligence and culture to his condition, than is anywhere described in the Bible. It is the impression conveyed by most statements upon the subject in our Confessions and theological systems.

Deistical writers have used this assumption in decrying the Biblical account, ever since Lord Kames took the lead more than a century ago in his "Sketches of the History of Man." But especially since the principle of evolution has gained scientific establishment, it is claimed boldly that man's fall from the highest perfection in Adam, supposed to be taught in the Scriptures, reverses the true fact.

The "New Theology," sometimes called Progressive Theology, that has recently loomed up, proclaims the story of Adam a *myth*, to be classed with the vague and preposterous traditions that are found in the prehistoric literature of various nations of antiquity. The grounds of this judgment seem to lie partly in a dislike to the doctrine of the imputation of Adam's sin to his posterity, especially in the arbitrary nominalistic conception which some eminent dogmaticians find in the Westminster Catechism, and partly, or even more, in the apparent impossibility of reconciling the account in Genesis with an evolution in man, and in everything pertaining to his sphere of being, of an ascent from lower to higher, from germinal to mature, from savagery to civilization, presumably to end in perfection, but beginning with the life of the beast.

As for the former of these reasons for disparaging Adam, we may retain our belief that he is a veritable historic personage, yet easily free ourselves from all metaphysical entanglements connected with the imputation of his sin, by statements that would be out of place here.

With reference to *evolution*, while we need Adam as embodying the race-idea so important in Biblical Theology, we also need him—the very Adam described in Genesis—as the beginning of evolution in man in his marvellous history under the divine formative energy, which it is rightly claimed, whether by infidel or progressive Christian, began very low.

The idea of a highly developed perfection in Adam is an assumption not warranted by the record. It has been singularly misread. We may not like to call him a savage, but certainly he was not civilized. His life must have been the most primitive and simplest imaginable. What distinguished him from the brutes around was some quality, attribute, or function called *likeness to God*, and produced by the divine breath animating the material structure.

The basis of this divine likeness, like the canvas of the painter or the marble on which the sculptor executes his beautiful conceptions, is the self-conscious personal intelligence called *soul*,—of which we have already spoken as finding its appropriate sphere in material things,—in living union with the higher moral capacity called *spirit*, which absorbs and reflects the beauty of God's moral perfections.

A grand nature truly, if it may ever attain its growth. No doubt under favorable conditions it might have been rapidly developed, both in soul and spirit—or more intelligibly to many persons, and with sufficient accuracy, both in mind and heart—into a glorious perfection.

But at first the higher principle was a mere breath, an impartation of divine life, but in weakness and not in power. One not aware of its exalted origin and immortal nature might suppose it would immediately expire, like a breath of man. Everything indicates that it was the feeblest conceivable entity, germinal and infantile. It was of so delicate quality that any willing contact with sin must blight it, its beauty and glory must disappear, and man immediately becomes a savage, probably of lower order than anything that we know by that name in this advanced stage of the world's history.

Adam was remarkable, not so much for what he was, as for what was possible to his nature; and he transmitted to the race all the rudimentary undeveloped potencies of that nature, embryonic, blighted, and ineffective, except by a fresh infusion of spiritual life and vigor from the original source. Nevertheless, the bestowment was most precious as distinguishing him from the beast, and securing to him a grand future whenever God's time shall come.

Let us not think of this story as a *myth*. It is a heathenish word that classes this invaluable Scripture account with "profane and old wives' fables" (Gr. *myths*) in the only New Testament passages in which myths are mentioned.* We must know this Adam, whether inspired parable, or literal historic fact, if we would know ourselves—where we stand and what we may hope for—and achieve a glorious future through the principles that underlie this realistic narrative.

If ever there was a radiant inspiration elsewhere than in the Lord's Anointed, who in important respects was the counterpart of the Adam of Eden, it is here. It may be mentioned that in the progressive theology of the writer's maturing life, the account of the creation and fall of Adam, referred to so slightingly by later progressives, has been an illumination that sheds its lustre down the whole history of redemption. It shows what man originally was, at least germinally and potentially, what he became through the blight of separation from God, and what must be done for him by divine grace, if he is ever to attain his full stature.

Personally we are content to receive the description as a detail of literal transactions. Yet we do not care to press it in extreme literalness upon others. Let "the dust" of which Adam was made, stand for any crude, inorganic matter, from which,—directly or indirectly, whether through a long series of animal transformations beginning at the lowest, or by an immediate creative act,—his body was produced.

Here, for aught we know to the contrary, may be-

---

* 1 Tim. i. 4; 1 Tim. iv. 7, 2 Tim. iv. 4; Tit. i. 14; 2 Pet. i. 16.

long "the men of the drift," the "cave-dwellers," and their like, the slayers of the mammoth and the mastodon and other monstrosities of the primeval world, the 'missing link' between the race of Adam and all lower animal types, men in structure and in modes of activity and life, but without the divine breath, and hence without spiritual perception, moral responsibility, or immortal existence, and swept away by convulsions in the frame of nature. There is wide room for unrecorded development in the sentence that describes the creation of our progenitor. Compression in time, with description of long processes as momentary, is characteristic of the whole narrative.

As for other items in the account, let *"the breath of life,"* as breathed into him by the Creator, be admitted an anthropomorphism, the most expressive exponent and symbol of the highest life as divinely imparted. It surely can be nothing more, and nothing less. Let the prohibitive ordinance, "*Thou shalt not eat of it*," represent tropically some very simple and reasonable restraint upon sensual appetite by which the nature could be tested and strengthened, and assume for "*the serpent*" any supposable seductive agency from without.

What myth of any nation presents features of ethical probability to be compared with this? If one choose to think of it as idealized fact, of the nature of parable, allegory, or symbolic statement, as essential history in a figurative dress, as object-teaching in which great ethical realities are exhibited in imaginative form, it is all we have occasion for. It is a story surcharged and redolent with the highest inspiration. We have very little respect for the sagacity that can see in it only a myth, in a line with the confused, monstrous, and unmeaning legends of heathenism.

But now, in connection with the revelation of truth relating to the higher life, especially as embracing a more perfect knowledge of God, profound problems are reaching the surface; what was hidden in darkness comes up from unfathomable depths. We are learning why all revelation of the deep things of God was normally gradual, progressive, shining more and more to the full-orbed noonday. God here, as everywhere, works from within in steadfast advance toward an ideal, not only in the outer world, but in man, his living image. It all leads to a bright outshining in the far-away future.

We shall claim more distinctly by and by, that *the production of a perfect humanity*, at first in an individual, and afterward through him in the race—the development of the latent potencies in Adam, in spite of all opposition of evil from whatever source,—*is the ruling purpose of the whole revelation*, and gives character and method to the inspiration that produced it. Let this be remembered. It is worthy to be amplified in its place.

Man was made by God of "the dust of the earth," however remotely in relation to the crowning act, and was endowed as we have seen with a nobler life than any upon the earth before him, but he was made to grow. Not only the individual man Adam, as the type generic of every individual man, but the nature as the concrete product of an expansive living force within, was made to grow.

Even the higher principle within him was originally evolved—through evolution of superior sort to that of things physical and material, and of natural law—a living person from a living personal God. And the inner connection between the originating and the originated nature,—the link of life, and growth, and power,—has never been severed. It holds within it the principle of immortality, of moral purity, and of all high excellence, if by any means in the power of God its normal condition can be restored.

There was a loss, a fall, a sad deterioration, probably almost immediate, and it resulted in injury apparently irreparable. The higher principle, the moral faculty, the capacity for fellowship with God, which it seemed must secure to him rapid progress and complete development, was miserably blighted. Progress in the higher direction was arrested, and unless infinite wisdom should exhibit some new method, arrested for all time.

It is in accordance with all analogies in moral renovation by fresh communication of truth, that if man is thus restored, the renovating truth must first be grasped, at least in the signification of the language in which it is conveyed, by his intellectual and rational faculties, as a medium of communication with the inner and higher life. Each principal element in his supra-bestial organism has its own capacity for growth, and under divine tuition will be cared for in accordance with its nature and laws. The spiritual, or more divine of the two, has not become extinct. New life from the original source may and shall be infused.

But the growth of soul, the exterior, and of spirit, the interior capacity for receiving fresh truth, must ordinarily be proportional and symmetrical. As it was said by ancient scientists, "Nature abhors a vacuum," we Theists may say more correctly, God abhors the abnormal and unshapely.

What we call, speaking humanly, *a law of nature*, describes the unfettered and intelligent course of infinite wisdom—the soul and spirit of creation, and as well, of the providential government of the world, including its moral transformation. One of the so-called laws secures the parallel and co-ordinate development of the several capacities of the complex humanity, which he will not abandon.

We need these statements here in laying down first principles on which all progress in knowledge and goodness must depend, in direct connection with the creation of the first man. We shall need them more as we advance, and shall refer to them again.

XIV.

HOPE LONG DEFERRED.

ARE we not approaching in the foregoing statement the probable explanation of the long delay in the production upon the earth of the ideally perfect man, the seed of the woman and the Son of God?

There has been much wondering over the protracted postponement of God's gracious purpose toward the world in the final and perfect revelation. Everything moved so slowly. Generations, centuries, decades of centuries passed away, kingdoms rose and fell, religions and philosophies appeared, culminated, and collapsed, yet the promise still waited.

We are told that "the fulness of time" must first come. Some indispensable but undefined preparation must be completed. Meanwhile, how frequently the entire population of the earth was changed. Myriads of millions passed off into eternity without the knowledge of the true God or the hope of immortality.

The thought is painful beyond conception—one under which nothing but the strongest confidence in the almighty, all-wise, and all-merciful rule of a divine will can steady our reeling souls—that so many generations had to perish in darkness. It could not have been an arbitrary exhibition of sovereignty on the part of the great Supreme. Why could not the promised deliverer, the "Hope of Israel," have appeared at the farthest a century or two after man's ruin, revealing the highest heavenly truth that greets our hearts in the New Testament, and bringing life and immortality to light?

The best work on progressive revelation, especially in its bearing upon the point now under consideration, is Canon Mozley's "Ruling Ideas in Early Ages, and their Relation to Old Testament Faith." We give the scope of the book with great freedom in the following sentences, leaving it for subsequent consideration to what extent and in what way, if at all, its leading thought needs to be modified or supplemented in its relation to New Testament revelation and faith: A religion from God, embodying the highest conceptions, and opening up before men a glorious future of knowledge, purity, love, and blessedness in divine fellowship, must be revealed progressively. If it had been at once proclaimed in its higher and purer form, men in their moral darkness and degradation could not have received it. It must come to them through their own moral atmosphere, and modified by its obstructions, misapprehensions, and confusion on all ethical questions. It could only be apprehended gradually, as accommodated to the prepossessions which must for an indefinite time shut out the perfected and absolute truth and right. So modified, it might by degrees effect a moral transformation, rectify unworthy conceptions of God, elevate the ethical standard, and lift the race to a higher plane.

From this vantage-ground a fresh revelation of the justice, holiness, and love of God as crystallized in a perfect man, the representative head of redeemed humanity, could be apprehended, appreciated, embraced, and absorbed, and thus the whole mass should be changed into the image and likeness of God in all moral perfections.

The view contemplates the certainty in an earlier revelation of an admixture of the true and the false, the divine conception tarnished or discolored by the imperfect medium through which it must reach the hearts of men. Canon Mozley exhibits the facts on which his statements are based at some length, proving conclusively that he is not dealing in vain speculations, or in fancies that can never be realized.

In successive chapters he takes up some of the principal examples that occur in the Old Testament of divine commands that are not in harmony with the New Testament standard of right and wrong. After a lecture upon Abraham, as introducing a new and pure religion, he treats in several lectures of the commanded sacrifice of Isaac,—of exterminating wars as ordered by God,—of the visitation of the sins of the fathers upon the children,—of the killing of Sisera by Jael, and the treachery of her act,—of the law of retaliation, and under it, of the justice executed by "the avenger of blood."

He shows that in all these there is a temporary accommodation in matters of justice, love, and truth to the infirmities of men, and that this has its origin in the condescension of God in becoming the Guide and Instructor of a people whose moral apprehensions were imperfect, although they were not without a confused sense of religious obligation, righteousness, and truth.

Canon Mozley does not distinctly raise the question whether in the nature of things and absolutely the slow progress was unavoidable,—whether by a new exercise of creative power, an omnipotent reconstruction of man's moral nature, God might not at once have lifted him to a higher level, from which the most perfect truth and right could have been clearly and correctly discerned. It is enough that the great Ruler of all chose to act in accordance with the established analogies of creation and providence, in which time is of small moment, and from which haste is banished as an element of weakness. He preferred for good and sufficient reasons to accomplish his gracious purpose by moral methods, exhibiting his infinite wisdom in multitudinous details.

So we might infer that he would have done from all past records in the kingdom of nature. He would exhibit his grace in righting all wrong and expelling all evil, but there should be no rude shock, throwing the race off its balance by a sudden revolution in all accepted ethical notions. The truth should win its way, and achieve supremacy over the hearts and lives of men in its purest form, by entering gradually into the current of human thought and practice. Thus by degrees, but surely, it must eliminate the elements of weakness and obscurity embedded in the nature of those with whom God is now graciously dealing.

The following analysis of Canon Mozley's Tenth

Lecture, "The end, the test of a progressive revelation," as given in the Table of Contents, is most suggestive: " Answers to objectors to the foregoing argument—A progressive revelation may make use of imperfect moral material—It looked forward—An inward mind in the system taught *ex cathedra*—The prophets—The end shows the design of the system—While accommodating itself to defective ideas, it was eradicating them—No system of philosophy taught the rights of man—The Bible the charter of man's rights—Ancient empires flourished on the insignificance of man—The vast body of philosophy and poetry formed by the Bible—Pascal—Great body of infidel literature formed on the same idea—Shelley—The communion of man with God affected the relation of man with man—The law thus contained the secret of his elevation—History shows the law to have been above the nation—The nation was terrified into a formal obedience—The enforcement of law the task of one generation, its fruits of another—A progressive revelation must be judged by its end—Higher minds outgrew the law of their dispensation—Other nations stopped short—In the Jewish nation alone the law acted as a guide—The great prophetic order—The objector asks, Why should divine revelation be subject to conditions?—The human will, its capacity of resistance—The whole question belongs to the fundamental difficulty of reconciling God's power with man's free will—Miracles—Temporary morals only a scaffolding."

It cannot be questioned that Canon Mozley has rendered important service to Biblical Theology in accounting for acts recorded in the Old Testament which exhibit a low standard of morality, yet seem to bear the seal of divine approval. In the Sermon on the Mount our Saviour strongly emphasizes the contrast between the principles of the Mosaic legislation, and those that emanate from his own higher authority: "It was said to you by them of old time, 'An eye for an eye and a tooth for a tooth'; but I say unto you, Love your enemies, do good to them that hate you, and pray for them that despitefully use you and persecute you." Elsewhere our Saviour speaks of a law of Moses as not such a genuine and perfect expression of the will of God as would have been given to people more susceptible to right impressions: "For the hardness of your heart Moses gave you this precept."

With this supreme endorsement in our mind we are not disturbed if any one should declare that some of the statutes in this ancient revelation would disgrace any modern system of laws. So it is set down in the "Mistakes of Moses." We may fitly and fearlessly admit this. There is no better way of depriving such sallies of rampant and indiscriminate infidelity of their power to hurt than by candid assent. For one greater than Moses has confirmed the assertion by finding in that law as a ruling principle, condescension to human infirmity.

Barbaric ideas were too thoroughly rooted in the thought and practice of those barbaric ages to yield even to the injunctions of a divine Lawgiver. But they might in his infinite wisdom be tolerated for a time in connection with a revelation whose higher elements were illuminative and regenerative. For thus, with some temporary permission of evil, the way might be prepared for that highest truth before which the whole mass of barbarism and heathenism should be swept from the earth.

The deficiency in Canon Mozley's treatment of the subject may be sharply illustrated by a personal incident. Several years ago, while spending a Sabbath in the forest, the writer of these sentences passed over the volume to a friend, without remark about its contents, but with a specific purpose. He was a man of mature, penetrative, and judicial mind, accustomed to weigh evidence, expose legal sophistries, and pronounce determinatively upon abstruse subjects; one not prepossessed by any theological system, and always ready to deal with commonly received opinions in an independent way. He returned it in an hour, with the quiet question, "Is not that view fatal to the scheme of modern Christian missions?" The reply was equally quiet, simply expressing a different opinion, and the subject was dropped without discussion.

The question was shrewd, and touched a vital point. It seemed to have been seized with some avidity, not as against Canon Mozley's argument, but as against the hopefulness of taking the advanced truth of the Gospel to the more benighted regions of heathendom. There are tribes now upon the earth that are supposed to be as ignorant and debased as the old Canaanites. On what ground can we discriminate? Why must we not go back to the old system, beginning with the sacrifice of beasts as the mode of worship, and lowering our moral instruction wherever we find it necessary, in accommodation to their savagery and barbarism? The inference from the ruling principle of the book as we have stated it, was not illegitimate.

The author concentrated his thought rigidly and too exclusively upon his principal topic, and does not seem to have connected it very distinctly in his own mind with the possibilities or the facts of the far-away future. He proceeded upon the assumption that in dealing with deep moral debasement there were imperative and controlling reasons for adopting this protracted educational process, and that no other could have been effective. He does not ask whether it succeeded or failed, whether the remote descendants of those favored with the earlier revelation advanced so far in knowledge and subjection to the divine will, that when fuller illumination visited the world, they absorbed it joyfully, and became the loving and obedient sons and daughters of the living God. He seems to take it for granted that such must have been the issue, or that in some unexplained way it extended to the whole body of mankind. Nothing can be clearer than that this was contrary to fact.

Neither does Canon Mozley ask whether the ever-energetic wisdom and grace of God might not in the future evolve a more penetrative, potent, and effective agency, which should supersede the superficial and imperfect methods that alone were possible at first,—that should illumine, regenerate, develop, and transform the most degraded and morally obtuse,—that by working subjectively and *ab intra*, should attain results by rapid progress which under the previous system had not been realized after centuries of objective and extrinsic training. The prophecies of the Old Testament evidently contemplate this most distinctly.

Yet the provisional divine method adopted at the beginning was not altogether fruitless. Important purposes were accomplished. The history of the people so signally distinguished shows advance in divine knowledge, some clearer apprehension of truth and obligation, as generation succeeded generation. The worship of the true God and the instruction and warnings of his prophets were not all in vain. As for the rest, the divine originator of the earlier system must have known full well the obdurate nature of the personal material he had to deal with, and the inadequacy of all extrinsic methods of subduing the evil inclinations of men. If nothing more could have been accomplished, it was something to prove beyond controversy for all the future the absolute need of truth in such form, and instinct with such inherent, penetrative, and quickening spirit and life as should overcome all resistance and reanimate the dead.

Besides this, during that long interval, an invaluable body of imperishable truth obtained lodgment and expression in the earth, addressed to whomsoever it might concern, to be appropriated, enjoyed, and utilized for human need in all the future. Those who came first might serve, if they cared for nothing more, as common carriers to the generations to come. And through all those ages a highway was being cast up for the coming of the great King. A descent was provided from a royal and favored stock for the seed of promise whose word and power should bring joy to the nations. Human thought, too, was broadened and deepened by the earlier revelation, and so by necessarily slow process a language was formed, rich and copious, which, better than all the tongues that had ever been known among men, could express the living truth that should bring the fallen and lost into fellowship with God.

We are not at a loss for an answer to the sceptical question so naturally suggested by Canon Mozley's otherwise admirable work, with regard to the hopefulness of carrying the advanced truth of the Gospel, the perfected wisdom and grace, to the nethermost pagan mind. It might be enough for us, who recognize a divine Commander-in-chief with full confidence and joyful submission to his will, to say that we do not care to speculate and philosophize. We are under positive orders. We have the command to go into all the world and preach the Gospel to every creature, which includes Hottentots and cannibals—all degrees of moral obtuseness—and he guarantees our success by his assurance, "I am with you always, even to the end of the world." Hearing this word, neither prophet nor apostle, canon nor cardinal, philosopher, jurist, nor pope shall turn us aside.

We add to this that incontestable facts are better than philosophical assumptions. The living word of Christ, which it is our desire in this little book above all things to exalt, does penetrate the brutish heart. It is showing its power in the everyday experience of thousands, who, in faith and love and deepest sympathy with men in their spiritual blindness and degradation, are putting it to the test, and have abundantly proven its effectiveness. It was only yesterday that one of our most cultured citizens, a man of keen observation, but not a Christian at all, who had just returned from Honolulu, told us of having visited an old patriarch of great intelligence, thoroughly civilized, in all his thoughts and ways like one of us, who distinctly remembered the debasing human sacrifices, and the horrid superstitions and cruelties of a population so recently savage and barbarous, but who now, transformed by the Gospel within a single generation, desire to come into closest bonds with ourselves.

We only need further to ask,—whatever may be alleged of the earlier divine method, as contradicting every other hope of elevating the debased,—what encouragement have we to go back to a system which proved so ineffective in laying hold upon the hearts of men, when we have in our possession the living words that "millions have found to be the power of God unto salvation." If the perfected truth in the Gospel were an abstruse system of ethics and dogma, requiring faculties thoroughly trained by science and philosophy, we might indeed be hopeless of the results of missionary labor. But the glory of the Gospel is the simplicity of its message. It announces a Saviour whose lips give law to the world, and that law is love. It celebrates in all the earth the simple fact that "God so loved the world, that he gave his only begotten Son, that whosoever believeth on him should not perish, but have eternal life." It is a permanently effective revelation, which supplements or supersedes everything provisional or inadequate that had preceded it. The power it introduced into the world is vested in a divine person incarnate, who gives eyes to the blind and draws men to himself by a marvellous attraction. The time is come when the dead hear the voice of the Son of God, and hearing they live.

With the exception noted, the work of the eminent Oxford Professor is of rare value as a contribution to Biblical Theology. It is masterly in its moral discriminations, and in its clearness and force in exhibiting the consummate wisdom which gradually displaced the crude and unworthy conceptions that before held the ground, by a revelation at first fragmentary and imperfect, but step by step tending toward completeness. The view is illuminative, and we are prepared to carry the principle of progression as characteristic of God's dealings with the human race beyond the point where the writer has left it. By pressing his thought further in the same direction he might have brought a stronger light to bear upon the training of a debased humanity by divine methods to the highest moral excellence.

So, too, he might have solved more completely the mystery of the long delay before the dawn of Christianity; and the no less oppressive mystery of its slow progress after its introduction. Even yet to human appearance how far in the future is the completed moral restoration of our race—even yet now, after added centuries, in the indefinite future.

Infinite wisdom alone is fully adequate to these problems. If we venture a single step forward it may be thought that we are entering a region of abstractions and uncertainties. Dogmatic affirmation is certainly to be avoided.

Our principal relief is in facts already emphasized, —in the relation between the lower intellective faculty in man, and the higher spiritual nature, the breath of God, which alone can apprehend and enjoy him.

Is not truth, the aliment which in its separable elements must nourish both the lower and the higher, adapted to a twofold need? We may also recall from a previous chapter that in our personal apprehension of truth as revealed in the Scriptures, there is an evolutionary principle, a law of growth, which through the grace of the Spirit regulates the whole process of development in the individual and in the race. The truth lies before us in inexhaustible supply. But its reception and assimilation depend upon personal capacity. We refer now to the higher truth, to that which pertains to the infinite God in his relations with man as reaching the higher spiritual nature, the divine *pneuma*, through the intellect, the human *psyche;* for even spiritual truth has its intellective side.

Now what if there be here, not only a provision of appropriate fare for each constituent of our dual nature, as each hungers for truth of its own kind, but also a law, that the provision, and the consequen growth of the two, shall be equable; or, at least, that the higher shall not proceed much faster than the lower, which is mediately the source of its supply.

Thus would be secured the symmetrical development of the superior immortal nature from stage to stage in an ever ascending scale. Surely its advance must be relative; that is, relative to the more or less advanced intellective faculty, to which the aliment for both, the knowledge objectively supplied, will ever be adapted.

No one will question that there are certain correct statements concerning God, the loftiest subject of our human intellection, which are not above the reason, however narrowly defined. Even in its lowest condition it may be educated to their level by natural process. These statements are in a great measure abstract and juiceless, destitute of the spirit and life which cold and heartless reason cannot appreciate, nor even discern. Nevertheless they are true, invaluable, and also indispensable as a vehicle, or solvent — a chemist would say — through which the more profound, perfect, and spiritual knowledge must be received. They may be embodied in confessions and catechisms, to be recited by rote and accepted as articles of faith, and not altogether unintelligently. The learner may think that he knows God — and does he not in a very important sense? St. Paul refers to such knowledge in exhibiting the responsibility of the Gentiles as commensurate with their intelligence: "Because that which may be known of God is manifest in them; for God manifested it unto them. For the invisible things of him, since the creation of the world, are clearly seen, being perceived through the things that are made, even his everlasting power and divinity; that they may be without excuse" (Rom. i. 19, 20. R. V.).

Yet all along the line of human progress the truth presented concerning God, both in substance and form, must be wisely adjusted to undeveloped capacity, intellectual and spiritual. By a process of moral assimilation it enters the organism for which it was prepared, milk for babes and solid food for the mature.

The form, through the imperfection of the human medium of transmission, may exhibit some perversion, in which its higher and more potent elements are not manifest. But it may be, for that reason, the best possible for the organism at the time. By and by it will have enlarged capacity, and the same revelation may exhibit the full truth, through the more perfect conception in spiritual maturity.

XV.

HOPE LONG DEFERRED—CONTINUED.

This is a point of great interest in connection with the progressive education of the race under divine tutelage. It needs space, and we arrest for a few pages our advance in the main line.

We shall never penetrate the mystery of the protracted postponement of the revelation of Jesus Christ as the power of God unto salvation, and of other postponements that stagger weak faith, without a more profound study of man's composite nature,—of the two elements in its composition as restated in the last chapter, and of the relation of the superior principle or organ through which alone he can attain a true conception of God, to the inferior intellective faculty which is its basis, or indispensable prerequisite. Without the soul, or rational principle, as well as the spirit, or capacity for higher realities, the divine Spirit could never have entered into his being, bringing him into fellowship with God. The rational principle, as first in existence, may be thought of as the receptacle of the spiritual, as the latter is the receptacle of the pure and living truth of God in its higher significance and power. For here the conscience and all gracious affections have their seat, and in these God establishes his benign and loving authority and rules over the man.

In the nature of things there can be no revelation of God to a beast. The difficulty is similar in kind to that of teaching science to one of the stones of the field. Creative power must first produce *mind*. If one of the higher sciences is to be taught, it must have, as the indispensable preparation, mind in corresponding culture and advancement. It would be very meagre knowledge of astronomy that could be imparted to a Hottentot fresh from his native kraal by the most experienced and skillful educator. The requisite faculty is there, but it must be developed by methods appropriate to its nature and laws.

In the analysis of manhood in its completeness each component part rises higher than its precursor in the order of creation and existence,—body—soul—spirit. This order cannot be reversed, nor the intermediate constituent be omitted, so that the third may exist and perform its functions independently of the second. Neither can that intermediate be insufficient in culture and development, if spiritual truth of exalted quality and grade is to be successfully injected. When the intellectuality is feeble and narrow, only the rudiments of divine knowledge can be apprehended, and these very imperfectly. The deficiency may be called phenomenally lack of 'spiritual apprehension.' But the trouble is in part lower down in the human organism. For spiritual apprehension can never be wholly independent of the underlying intellectual apprehension, but must in some measure keep pace with it. For in the natural constitution and original scheme and order of divine efficiency, it was its crowning efflorescence and glory.

Whenever the intellect has attained sufficient growth we may expect a corresponding enlargement of the higher spiritual capacity through the impartation of new life from the primal source. This in its turn will create a stimulative reaction. The higher faculties in their development will expand and elevate the lower, and the whole man will rise to nobler rank in existence. This is abundantly confirmed by the frequent result of the entrance of spiritual life into men of low intellectuality.

Nevertheless it remains true, and should be held in remembrance with reference to our further statements upon the subject, that there must be some sufficient development of the lower intellectual capacity, in order that the salutary process may begin. Corroborative of this on a large scale, and helpful in the study of human nature in its bearing upon the mystery we are now contemplating, are the experiences of missionary activity when carried on extensively, and for a sufficient time. They are especially interesting as showing the development and expansion that result from the attempt to convey spiritual conceptions to comparatively low intellection.

The introduction of Christianity into the Turkish Empire serves our purpose admirably. It had mighty influence upon thought, language, and all educational advance, quite apart from success, or rather, with almost entire failure, in displacing the religious ideas of Mohammedanism and making converts to the new faith.

The first translation of the Bible into Turkish, although the best then possible, was very poor. This was simply because that language had no suitable words for some of the most important conceptions in the divine revelation. When complete, the translators gave it forth, earnestly endeavoring to convey to such as were accessible some right notions of God, and of the nature of the service he requires, in contrast with the religion of the Koran.

They succeeded in attracting attention and in stimulating intellectual activity. In some imperfect degree they were understood. But even the most elementary instruction upon such subjects, introduced many ideas quite foreign to previous thought. Immediately new words had to be forged, adapted to ideas less material and earthy than had been ever before conceived. The new faith was freely discussed *pro* and *con* in various circles. The prevailing opposition to its vaguely apprehended doctrines pressed forward the national mind, and enlarged its capacity for conceiving and expressing this elevated thought, this new philosophy concerning the nature of God, and his relations with men.

In less than ten years the first translation of the Scriptures became intolerable, simply because it was not up to the times. The nation had outgrown it, and this through its own educative influence,—a beautiful instance of evolution in the world of mind. Many new and expressive words had come into current use in matters ethical, metaphysical, and dogmatic, which were suggested by this book. Yet they were not found upon its pages, but in place of them words singularly inappropriate. Both thought and speech had so far transcended it, that it seemed fairly barbarous, and must be thoroughly rewrought in a fresh rendering.

The change went on. Newspapers, educational institutions of higher and lower grade, and other indications of intellectual advance increased and multiplied. The entire nation felt the pulsations of a new life in all departments of mental activity. The language continued to become richer in words adapted to the higher culture, especially in philosophic and religious thought. Even the second translation of the Bible in another decade became antiquated through the progress of education, and was supplanted by a third.

It makes the fact we are impressing more significant that through the rigorous exclusiveness and intolerance of Mohammedanism, the essential principles of Christianity as a spiritual religion failed to produce any appreciable effect upon the religious life of the nation during all this time.

We can begin now to understand how it was that the higher inspiration and more perfect revelation of God, that were to transform the world, might not be introduced until due preparation had been made in the intellectual growth of humanity. This preliminary result has been measurably secured by various natural processes ordained by infinite wisdom and grace. At first, in families, or groups of families, constituting a tribe or nation, in close relation and mutual dependence on interchange of thought. Then further, by enlargement of ideas through the contact of every nation with a world outside its own limits; by philosophies propounded and controverted; by the more extended knowledge of monotheistic Judaism with its rich traditional knowledge of the earliest time, and its exalted religious theory and practice in contrast with surrounding heathenism,—by these and many other influences, the range of thought became wider and deeper, and the mind of the world was steadily rising somewhat nearer the level it should normally attain if the higher truth is to root itself in the mind of the world. Otherwise, in the course of nature it must soon have perished, like the seed sown in stony places where it had not much depth of earth.

What we have thus advanced is confirmed by the results of missionary labor in India. We refer to intellectual and religious ferment within the last fifty years, in connection with the British rule in India, and the contact of its vast population with Christianity. It is a well-known fact that the ancient beliefs are losing their hold upon the leading native races. The great problem is, what shall replace them? The foolishness of Hinduism with its Shastras has been outgrown. From the old Vedas, produced in the long-past age when Sanskrit was a living tongue, come deep-toned echoes confirmative of the truth of the Bible that human nature is corrupt, and evil continually. Their religion is a philosophy acute and profound. Whatever truth it contains is from God, an inspiration coincident with natural law in the development of an immortal spirit. But their highest wisdom exhibits no deliverance from the bondage and misery of sin, and as a system of religion it is doomed, as insufficient for the needs of men.

It is the testimony of a distinguished advocate of the new Brahmoism that "Christian missionaries, Christian men, and Christian literature above all, have roused the dormant nature of the East, the natural results of which are more or less manifest in every part of India." The principal natural result of this awakening is a rapid intellectual development, preparing the way, we may hope, for the clearer apprehension and more intelligent adoption of the spiritual religion of the Bible.

Yet the older faith of the Hindus had its glimpses of God and sporadic jewels of truth. So had the Confucian in China, the Zoroastrian in Persia, and the Olympic of Greece.* The "light of Asia," although not "the true light," "the light of the world," was not black darkness. For ages the preparation had been going on. Before Christianity was known to the inheritors of these ancient religions, and even in the far-off times when their great prophets were living instructors of men, the evolutionary process, intellectual and moral, however slowly, was already on the advance. Their oracles, now treasured as sacred, were not in the first instance delivered to antediluvian monsters,

---

* See Sir William E. Gladstone in *North-American Review*, April, 1891; "The Olympic Religion," No. III.

nor to the freebooting tribes of Abraham's time, nor to the degraded people that afterward polluted the soil of Canaan. Several thousand years make some difference in development under whatever disadvantages.

Everything moves faster now. The world is being more rapidly prepared for Christ, and Christ is coming forward to take possession of the world. God in nature, working from within its great heart toward a grand consummation, and the God of grace, proclaiming himself in Christ and the Bible, are one God, to be blessed forever. The natural and the supernatural are not so wide apart as some people imagine.

We have written these last pages as we might if the whole world had enjoyed the benefit of the process they briefly describe,—of the impact of mind upon mind that has stimulated the intellectual, and to some extent the moral, activities of the principal races of the earth. We need not be reminded that outside of this current and flow, on distant shores and islands of the sea, and in the interior of great continents, there are isolated tribes of a lower type, unaffected by the upward tendency of the central mass. Their barbarism and moral debasement is scarcely less than that of the earliest historic times.

The conviction has been expressed in the chapter immediately preceding, that the great Supreme is not the bond-slave to his own prevailing methods. The processes of nature in the material universe are variable. Geological changes whose time must ordinarily be measured by immense periods, may be wrought by the greater activity of natural forces most rapidly. In the freer evolution of the world of spirit, of intelligence, of personal will, as between the great Supreme and those into whom he has breathed his own life, there are all hopeful possibilities through special grace for special need. The labors of Williams in the South Sea Islands, and of Moffat in Southern Africa, are the abundant proof of the power of the Gospel to transform the most degraded.

XVI.

THE PURPOSE OF THE REVELATION.

WE have now reached the last of the several points that were proposed in the tenth chapter. It was there stated that whatever is necessarily implied in revelation as a gracious activity, must be helpful in defining the inspiration that produced it. It implies nothing more clearly than a specific purpose in the mind of the Revealer, to the accomplishment of which the revelation will be adapted in measure and in form.

We could not avoid the incidental mention of this divine purpose in remarking upon the Scriptures as revealing God in his relations with men, and further in referring to the revelation as addressed definitely to the conscience and heart, and only to the intellectual perception as means to an end. Thus all the way along and at each successive step we have to choose between alternatives, and invariably have preferred the higher to the lower, the moral to the natural, the spirit to the intellect as chief in God's regard; and we must do so here with reference to the purpose of God in revealing himself to men.

In specifying this purpose we must distinguish between the *nearer* and the more *remote*, dwelling in this chapter upon the former.

THE PURPOSE OF REVELATION.

It may be assumed as self-evident that the purpose of any revelation must precisely correspond with its character and contents. For we have seen that the word *revelation* signifies literally the *putting aside a veil*, in order that whatever lies behind it may be seen and enjoyed in its practical uses and bearings. For what is a revelation that makes no one the wiser with reference to the subject it presents?

We have then our answer, since we know already that the subject of the disclosure is the infinite God in his righteousness and grace, as manifested in his dealings with the children of men. His transcendent moral excellences were unveiled before them, in order to a suitable impression upon their consciences with reference to his claim to their reverence, confidence, and obedience. He would fain reach their hearts, and establish there his gracious authority — that "with unveiled face beholding as in a mirror the glory of the Lord, they may be transformed into his image from glory to glory, even as by the Spirit of the Lord." Thus the exterior revelation becomes interior, now for the first a revelation indeed.

Such words as the following occur to us in illustration,—words of our Saviour: "I thank thee, O Father, Lord of heaven and earth, that thou hast hid these things from the wise and prudent, and hast revealed them unto babes. Even so, Father, for so it seemed good in thy sight." "Blessed art thou, Simon Barjonah; for flesh and blood hath not revealed this unto thee, but my Father which is in heaven";—and other words from St. Paul, forgetting his admirable dialectics, not speaking as a philosopher, or a theologian, but relating in simple words the most precious experience of his personal life, by virtue of which he became the power for good that he was: "It was the good pleasure of God who separated me, even from my mother's womb, and called me through his grace, *to reveal his Son in me*, that I might preach him among the Gentiles."

The light of holy love so revealed irradiates the house, and no evil thing can abide it. Foul birds of darkness take their flight, and the renovated spirit delivered from its sin rejoices in God. "This is life eternal, that they should know thee, the only true God, and him whom thou didst send, even Jesus Christ."

Does this reach correctively any prevailing misconceptions of the Bible? Does it negative any of our thoughts concerning its chief purpose?

The principal purpose of our Bible is not to give us immaculateness as respects every infinitesimal point to be embodied in the most perfect creed or System of Theology. As already intimated, the Sacred Volume has been treated too much as if it were a confused mass of heterogeneous material for the elaboration of a catechism. Undoubtedly the exercise of framing such symbols has stimulated, strengthened, and sharpened intellectual acumen amazingly, and has thus proved splendid training for that important part of our interior mechanism.

But we imagine that if such had been the divine purpose this great volume would have been considerably reduced in its dimensions, and that we should have found somewhere between its lids more definitions and something that looks more like a creed than anything that occurs there. What an abundant Confession of Faith might be compressed within the space now occupied by the four Gospels. Why should not the inspiring Spirit have helped us in this, instead of leaving the precious material so mixed and scattered that all the doctors cannot arrange and express some small parts of it to their unanimous satisfaction?

Was it the divine purpose, that those who love the Lord Jesus Christ and glory in him as the one living head of the one church that he built, should think alike on all points of doctrine, and that the now-called Arminians and Calvinists, Churchmen and Dissenters, Sprinklers and Immersionists, should occupy one fold, and recite with one heart and voice their common *Credo*, even as they expect hereafter to celebrate in unison the praises of redeeming love?

If this were so, never has a divine purpose failed so lamentably. Instead of uniting them in holy love and faith and praise, this intellective exercise upon the revelation they all hold divine has been the means of separating them, it seems almost hopelessly, unless God shall give us a new revelation as an exposition of the old.

And one might ask, Can there ever be a revelation in words about the meaning of which acute minds may not differ widely? It does not seem possible; and we have grievously misconceived and misused the

THE PURPOSE OF REVELATION. 143

precious Book that reveals to us the Father and the Son, in insisting on uniformity of creed in minute details as the most important of all things. The divine purpose must have been, we need not quote Scripture to prove it, to unite the heterogeneous mass of humanity in blessed fellowship, having one Lord, one faith, and one baptism. Is it possible that this shall ever become a realized fact?

It is the common cry in sustaining verbal inspiration against those who question it, How shall we otherwise know what to believe? As if everything precious were imperilled if any minute point in which these creeds differ should become doubtful; or as if the claim that inspiration is in the thought and substance, and not in the words, affected any Christian doctrine whatsoever. But surely it does not. It leaves the same material for the adroit dialectician, the profound philosopher, and the skillful systematizer with his perfected logical arrangements.

We promised something more in its place about Systematic Theology, in mitigation of apparent disrespect in alluding to its principle and methods, as in contrast with those in Biblical Theology, especially to its framework and order as mechanical and artificial, where the other is natural and living.

But it is a noble discipline. Our logical faculties are a divine gift, and no mean part of our original endowment. Dialectic ability is to be wisely and carefully trained, and used for the maintenance of truth, as it is by others for its demolition. Formula must be met by formula, and syllogism by syllogism.

144   THE PURPOSE OF REVELATION.

Sophistry must be exposed and put to shame by logical process more acute and discriminating.

This is its province, not to be disparaged—to establish truth by sound reasoning, to refute error when presented in the forms of logic, and to satisfy minds that are trained to abstract and philosophical thought, and are fond of metaphysical distinctions. Let it be cultivated, but always remembering that in so far as its range is metaphysical and philosophic, passing beyond the limits of common thought, it is for the theological class-room or for books addressed to metaphysicians and philosophers, or to theologians supposed to be such, and not for ordinary practical use in exhibiting the significance of the divine revelation for the general instruction of mankind.

Let it not be discarded as obsolete, but sedulously improved, especially by more careful and accurate study of the Bible. Already, while holding its separate place, it is more discriminative in its treatment of Scripture, as based on a sound exegesis, and a recognition of the different values of its material as indicated by Biblical Theology, less abstract and angular, more spirited and inspiring. It will be a grand theology soon, that we may all rejoice in. For every gain, and all growth in any one method of dealing with divine truth must be of interest to all others as conducive to their common purpose.

We return to the affirmative, but only for emphatic restatement.

The immediate purpose of the divine revelation in the Scriptures, as manifest from the beginning, is to

THE PURPOSE OF REVELATION.

reach and develop the moral sensibilities of men in their personal relation to a personal God, to renovate the character and life, to create confidence in place of distrust; that men may appreciate God at his true value to themselves, may cultivate friendship with him more sedulously than with one another; that desire and delight may come in, where before was apathy or aversion; that men may repent of their sin, and know, love, and obey the Father of their spirits.

And in order that such effects may be more surely produced, we have God revealed to us in the Scriptures, not in abstractions and refined theological subtleties, but in all gracious activity, as Sovereign and Father, an almighty Protector and Friend, to be loved and trusted forever.

These exhibitions are all independent of studied and unvarying phrase. The inspiration that created them was more of the heart than of the head. They are in pictures, rather than in words,—in thought, spirit, substance, and not in the letter.

The *remote* purpose of the Old Testament revelation is only accomplished beyond the historic limit of time within which its inspiration was confined. This will be considered more fully after an intervening chapter.

XVII.

THE GLORY OF THE OLD TESTAMENT REVELATION.

Say what we may of inaccuracies and contradictions, the divine element in these Hebrew Scriptures cannot be obscured or rationally denied. Above the broad surface of uninspired literary achievement it glows and flashes with a superior radiance. We forgive and forget in its enjoyment the ruthless Saracenic bigotry that destroyed the libraries of Cesarea and Alexandria. Those vast depositories of human erudition can have contained no treasures to be compared with this.

In the presence of this radiance we may think as its analogue of the constellary grouping of stars in the Milky Way, whose luminous arch, sweeping from horizon to horizon, seems to project in bold relief from the darkness on either side. As we gaze on this glory we may think of the Alps in the European landscape, sublimely towering above the low lying levels of Germany in one direction, and of Italy and the Mediterranean in the other.

Such is the Old Testament inspiration in which we rejoice. It is not that of the jot and the tittle, of vowel points and accents, of mint and anise and cummin, of microscopic microbes and infusoria. We see in it "the true light that lighteth every man, coming into the world," and little by little scattering the darkness that enveloped it. "The testimony of Jesus is the spirit of prophecy." What did the Apocalypt mean by that? "The Lord cometh, let the earth rejoice,—let the multitude of the isles be glad thereat. Clouds and darkness are round about him, righteousness and judgment are the supports of his throne."

In the presence of this light from heaven, where is your vain babbler, your meretricious, dramatic, juggling, scoffing sophist, who parades "The Mistakes of Moses," and thinks that he has obliterated the everlasting truth of God? But this shall endure, though all else that attracts our admiration should perish. Mortal man in his greatest glory and pride is like grass and the flower of the field. "The grass withereth, and the flower fadeth, but the word of the LORD abideth forever." And we confidently add the apostolic comment upon the old prophecy: "And this is the word that by the Gospel is preached unto you."

The Old Testament contains a revelation of incomparable value, not only to the chosen race to which it was imparted, but to all the world. But its value resides not in the accuracy of every date, and the coherence of its minor details with each other, and with the absolute truth; not in its escape from all injury through the blundering manipulation of its appointed custodians, who imagined themselves authorized to accommodate it to tradition in matters not affecting its ruling import and scope.

But its excellence and power are discovered in the record it contains,—one that may be fearlessly subjected to the severest tests of historic criticism,—the record of a divine ordering of events since the beginning of the world toward a glorious consummation in the bursting of light from heaven upon those sitting in the darkness and shadow of death,—of transcendent theophanies, God who made the heavens of old, now with gracious intent visibly manifesting his glory before the eyes of men,—of ordinances and institutions full to the brim of significance for the future, object-lessons of the most luminous kind which the great Teacher held up before his pupils,— of prophecies growing clearer and clearer from the day of temptation and sin till the "fulness of time" had come for the final and perfect revelation of God in the flesh, to which providential guidance, vision, theophany, type, and prophecy had steadily pointed from the first.

This revelation of grace was so thoroughly woven into these ancient records by the inspiring Spirit— woven into their texture and substance—that it could not be materially impaired except by the absolute destruction of the whole fabric. Mere surface changes, whether produced by ignorance or artifice, were of no consequence whatever. Its meaning for redemption, for moral impression, for encouraging to the faithful service of God and departure from sin, for inculcation of lessons of courage, hope, and confidence in God, was quite independent of chronological, geographical, or scientific exactness.

The traditions of the scribes and elders could do it no harm. They were too shallow to touch even the upper surface. "What is the chaff to the wheat, saith the LORD." Its sense might be given with the slavishness of extreme and barbarous literalism, or in sentences elegantly idiomatic and euphonious, or in the freest paraphrase in any language under heaven, yet its light, and spirit, and power were there, only less than should come in due time from the heart, and lips, and eyes, and life of him in whose glorious utterances and grace it all received its fulfillment.

What did it matter with respect to the hope of Israel to be realized in Christ, whether the earlier histories were written by Moses, or were the product of many minds, with the great lawgiver as author or editor only of a part? What did it matter whether the story of Eden were literal fact of the most prosaic kind, or fact idealized in condensed and graphic descriptions, for instruction concerning the early moral status of the race under the government of God? What did it matter whether the sweet singer of Israel wrote many Psalms, or only a few, after which others were modelled so like the Davidic that presently authorship became confused; and what matter whether these imitations of David belong to an early, or to a much later time than Jewish tradition has assigned them? What did it matter whether there were one Isaiah or two; or whether the Book of Jonah were historic fact throughout, or partly, like the parables of our Saviour, instructive fiction? What did it matter whether Moses personally gave the whole body of ritual enactments ascribed to him in the traditional Scriptures, or, as others hold, the Mosaic books contain, besides the original enactments, their fuller development by a fresh inspiration adapted to new circumstances and later needs? What did it matter if at some indefinite time long after these changes were introduced, the priests and scribes who had charge of this service, believing in an unwritten law, imagined that these later additions had been given upon Mount Sinai, and felt authorized to attach them to the original Mosaic legislation?

We may have our decided opinion upon any or all of these questions. It may be opposed to innovation upon the older views that have so long held the ground. We may maintain it stoutly. With regard to several of these questions our personal opinion tends strongly toward the conservative side. Yet whichever alternative we adopt, the light is all there, whose brilliancy no ignorance nor artifice can dim. God's holy truth is not endangered, nor can his merciful purposes be thwarted.

Our Saviour needed not in quoting from the Scriptures, nor in referring to them as fulfilled in himself, to correct errors in the current translation, nor in chronological arrangement, nor in reputed authorship. He needed not to trouble those to whom his burning words were addressed with the trivialities of Higher Criticism. He never did. Whatever might be the facts with regard to the questions which it raises, all the same he could say with unfaltering lips: "Search the Scriptures, for in them ye think ye

THE OLD TESTAMENT REVELATION. 151

have eternal life, and they are they that testify of me."

It will be observed that with reference to the inerrancy of the Old Testament, while we freely make admissions which some consider fatal, it is in the interests of truth, and for the maintenance of its divine authority. We do not abandon it to the enemy, as if its records of facts had been so thoroughly riddled and disparaged by historical criticism as to be no longer tenable; as if, dismantling our fortifications, and destroying our unavailing armament, we must retreat to safer ground. Making the most of obscurities and discrepancies, anachronisms and contradictions to secular history, they are indeed like specks in the marble pillars of the Parthenon, as compared with the thousand coincidences in minute circumstantial statement of historic incidents in the relations of the tribes of Israel to the nations around them. These are receiving astounding confirmation year by year from Egyptian and Assyrian research.

Yet not in these evidential contributions from without the commonwealth of Israel have the Scriptures their principal support. But in the continued existence of the Jewish nation,—the stewards of the living oracles of God, surrounded by mighty empires, with its bold and offensive testimony against their idolatries, and its worship of the one, living, personal Jehovah, the God of the Hebrews, as mightier than all their dynasties and their pantheons, and in its great luminous chain of historic, theophanic, and prophetic witness to the abiding grace of the

God of salvation, and of his sovereign purpose to raise up from the despised Hebrew nationality one stronger than all the kings and the gods of heathendom, who should deliver the earth from the curse of sin, and wear upon his head the crown of universal and everlasting dominion.

So again we echo the Apocalyptic voice: "*The testimony of Jesus is the spirit of prophecy.*" For it cannot be held too steadily before us, that this Old Testament is not self-luminous nor self-assertive. It shines with no dim lustre, yet with light other than its own. Alike in law and in history, as well in psalm as in prophecy, it is always looking forward, addressing itself even more to hope than to faith, and proclaiming the glory to come after.

It has its princes, potentates, and warriors, but its grandest majesty, its King of kings, lives outside its own limits. Its Christ, the anointed of God, on whose head are many crowns, is a foreshadowed Christ. Its golden age, its realized desire, its full fruition of joy and peace, are in the New Testament, in the historic Christ, the Son of God and the Saviour of the world.

The New Testament, in distinction from the Old, is *our own* revelation of God, that which as now living upon the earth, we may claim as our very own. The revelations of the far past belong to us only partially and indirectly; some, as promising what we now possess; some, as explanatory of the New Testament, where we might otherwise be at a loss about its meaning; some, as embodying general principles, which may sometimes be of use. But *here* we find the central life and light and truth, having which we might dispense with all other. While we have the sunlight we ask not for the starlight, except when our weak eyes need some relief from the excessive brightness of noonday.

This Christ of the Gospels is the completed revelation of God, the manifestation of divine righteousness and love, with which none can be compared, and which never can be surpassed.

XVIII.

THE PROPHETS—THE CHRIST—THE APOSTLES.

We pass over from the Old Testament to the New, from prophets to apostles; and between these two distinguished orders of men we behold one greater than them all; *the only perfect and final revelation of God to men.*

In the whole treatment of our subject, and in direct bearing upon the new definition we are seeking, there is no question so important as that which now confronts us. Our success in reconstruction depends upon the answer it shall receive: What is the relation of the revelation of God in Christ to all that preceded and followed it? What is the precise difference between this central form as revealing truth, and the inspiration of prophets on the one side, and that of apostles on the other?

As heretofore, we must not be too precipitate, but very carefully feel our way to a satisfactory result.

He comes at last. The long delay is ended. The "fulness of time" is reached. What is the significance of his coming? Who and what is he? What shall the world have henceforth that it had not already? Is it only a further and brighter illu-

THE APOSTLES. 155

mination—a fuller knowledge of God's holiness and grace?

If we give heed to prophetic intimations, the new revelation is in a person, rather than in words; in what he was and did, more than in what he said. What had to be done in the fulfillment of the promise of his coming? The head of the serpent must be bruised. The families of the earth must be blessed. A son of David must sit upon his throne whose kingdom shall be established forever. "Unto us a child is born; unto us a son is given; and the government shall be upon his shoulder: and his name shall be called Wonderful, Counsellor, The mighty God, The everlasting Father, The Prince of Peace."

God's *ultimate purpose*, now to be potentially realized, was *salvation*—the deliverance of the earth from the curse that blighted it. What does that mean? Is it only that some signal act of omnipotence is now to be expected, as if mountains were to be levelled and great gulfs to be filled—or all nature were to be transformed in ideal beauty and perfection? Somewhat so it had been pictured in prophecy, and it must come to that at last. But the facts we face first are simple and prosaic. Evil had taken possession of man's heart and ruled in his life. The Infinite God is set at naught, his law boldly transgressed, and his power defied. Something more than illumination, and other power than that which transforms nature, are required here.

One may ask with the completed Old Testament

in his hands, to what extent had that older revelation accomplished God's purpose in moral renovation? As a divine system of progressive education, it should have prepared its favored subjects for fuller disclosures of truth. Did it issue in this—so that satisfactory results may be expected from further illumination, simply and alone?

It must be replied to this question, that the grace of the Old Testament was not utterly ineffective. Some hearts were impressed. There were always in Israel devout worshipers and faithful servants of God. But comparatively very few,—one out of a thousand, or perhaps even fewer. The people as a whole were always blind and stubborn. The divine revelation shone steadily to the end brighter and still brighter. But as to immediate practical results, it did little for Israel, and nothing for the world at large.

Since words, whether addressed to the consciences or to the hearts of men, have all failed, something now must be *done*, thorough, emphatic, decisive. The revelation of God must be of a kind that shall mean something now which it did not before. Evil must be attacked at its seat and centre by a power greater than its own, and enslaved humanity set free.

But the deliverance must come from itself, *ab intra*, and not *ab extra*,—immanent, and not transcendent. The battle must be fought out on an earthly arena. The absolute evil and the absolute good must meet on the same level, foot to foot, face to face. And yet—figures of speech must not deceive us—the contest and victory depicted in the Gospel are fruitless, except so far as they are personally realized in individual need. A leaven must be infused into this human mass, that shall change its whole nature and substance. What is needed is not more light from without—that shall come too, as an indispensable coincident—but fresh power within, strength from God supplied to hearts morally weak, a new principle of life that shall bid defiance to death forever.

The problem is solved for us by the incarnation of Deity, by the eternal Word becoming flesh and dwelling among men. He grappled with the evil in the perfected glory of full-grown manhood in every faculty and fibre, yet in the power of God; mighty to save as God only can save, able nevertheless to sympathize with his human brotherhood in its moral imbecility and in all its imperfection—ready to suffer with it, ready to die for it. And he did die—"die unto sin," that men might "live unto God."

We can now answer the question: "Where and what was this perfect revelation in Christ in distinction from that of the prophets?" Radically different we now see; otherwise, like theirs, it would have been fruitless. It was not in words, as words; not on the line-upon-line principle; not in a more perfect rule of life; not in a creed, correct to an iota in every detail,—but in a divine, yet human, personality, love incarnate, truth incarnate, purity and moral perfectness incarnate, "bone of our bone, and flesh of our flesh," yet he did no evil, neither was guile found in his mouth. The divine purpose from the beginning is to be realized through an ideal manhood, the perfected Adam, from whom and in whom we have everlasting life.

We emphasize the answer. The revelation in Christ is not in words as words, but in a divine personality, and a power residing in that personality adequate to our redemption, and this power transmissible to us—yet *even in his words*, as the best expression of that personality to the centuries far forward—even in his words, higher than prophetic, higher than apostolic, higher than all possible human words, as the most perfect exponent of the moral power, immanent and transcendent, that shall stamp out evil forever.

It is in human accents that he speaks, but his words are the words of God, pure and undefiled. The fountain of wisdom whence they come is the same that lay behind the inspiration of the prophets. But their organs at the best were imperfect—their organs of perception and their organs of expression alike. They saw dimly. They spake feebly. They could not adequately translate for us the high thoughts of God into human speech. But he could, and he has. "The words that I speak unto you, they are spirit, and they are life." Yet not the words, as mere words; but as they become through the grace of the Spirit the principle of a new existence, the children of Adam becoming children of God.

Who and what upon the opposite side of the towering personality of Christ were the apostles? On a higher plane than the prophets surely, but subordinate to the chief revelation. Their work was glorious, but it was secondary. He did work such as none other man did, and they were his witnesses. It was his words that they rehearsed to the world. It was his life in all its phases that they described. It was his victory over sin and death by dying himself that they celebrated in all the world.

The message of the prophets was prospective, of the glory that should follow; that of the apostles retrospective, of the perfected glory of Christ. The one class pointed forward and the other back, but both to one higher than themselves. The one said, "He cometh," the other, "He came." "That which was from the beginning, that which we have heard, that which we have seen with our eyes, that which we beheld and our hands have handled of the word of life (for life was manifested, and we have seen, and bear witness, and declare unto you the life, the eternal *life* which was with the Father and was manifested unto us), that which we have seen and heard declare we unto you."

A goodly and blessed work was that of the apostles, an indispensable work, and for its accomplishment inspiration was indispensable. For the ultimate divine purpose was not exhausted in the incarnation, nor in the life, the gracious deeds, the suffering, the resurrection, the ascension of our Saviour. All these were means to an end. The power for salvation was there, but it must be brought to bear upon the world. Through them he sent forth his message of salvation to the remotest age. But they always spoke in *his* name, referred to his authority as supreme, and knew nothing but Christ, they his servants, and he their Master and their Lord.

We have the answer to our question, and shall use it presently. The revelation of God in Jesus the Messiah differs from all other, not only in degree, but in quality and kind. Prophets and apostles had nothing but what they received from him. He filled them with all they could contain, with all and more than they could impart. But he withheld vast treasures to be bestowed immediately, everywhere and always, without prophetic or apostolic intervention, upon those who come humbly to his feet.

XIX.
THE DISCRIMINATIVE DEFINITION IN PART.

HERE where it is most needed let us have before us an important conclusion we have reached. The character and purpose of the revelation must ever furnish the definition and measurement of the divine energy that produced it. The supernatural causation will be substituted for the natural only so far as shall be indispensable to the proposed moral effect.

In supplying material for a creed or confession, according to the modern idea of the necessary perfectness in all minor details of these boundary lines between different bodies of Christians, great precision is necessary. Almost verbal inspiration might be requisite in some places of extreme difficulty, especially in connection with matters abstract and metaphysical, in order to secure language that could not be misconceived.

Yet even here there are very few truths, none perhaps of special importance, which might not be stated in various language without danger of misconception. As a notorious fact, in places where definiteness would seem to be most important for confessional purposes, as for instance, in connection with points of doctrine which divide the Christian Church into sects, there is room for honest difference of opinion as to what the Scriptures that relate to them mean.

But in impressing a moral lesson by historic incident, in reaching the conscience, in moving the deeper religious sensibilities which stimulate and energize the will—which we have found to be the principal purpose of the revelation of God in the Scriptures—verbal inspiration could not be required. As for moral impression by historic statement, fiction is nearly as good as fact, or we should have no parables. For any ordinary use, the honest effort to ascertain the facts, and their statement with truthful purpose, is accepted as sufficient, even if some minor details are thought doubtful.

Our examination of the contents of the Bible in their diversity, and of the great variety of circumstances and characteristics of human existence to which they relate, has prepared us for a definition less compact, rigid, and inflexible than those which Systematic Theology usually requires and produces.

The inflexible definitions that confine the infinite Spirit of God within our narrow human measurements,—saying to him, Thus far shalt thou go, and no farther,—are to be studiously avoided. He is ever transcending the limitations we assign to him, casting off the trammels, asserting his liberty in the most practical way, and putting our sagacity to shame.

The following definition is intentionally copious. It has been made so comprehensive as to include the whole concrete result of inspiration exhibited in the Sacred Books, that is, the whole content and substance of Biblical Theology. Having the material spread out before us in its amplitude, it may be easy for any one so inclined to reduce its dimensions by omitting whatever he thinks least important to strict definition, in accordance with the tendency of the more scholastic theological systems to philosophical abstraction. But the practical design of this essay carries us in the opposite direction.

Inspiration is a special energy of the Spirit of God upon the mind and heart of selected and prepared human agents which does not obstruct nor impair their native and normal activities, nor miraculously enlarge the boundaries of their knowledge, except where essential to the inspiring purpose; but stimulates and assists them to the clear discernment and faithful utterance of truth and fact, and when necessary brings within their range truth or fact which could not otherwise have been known. By such direction and aid, through spoken or written words, in combination with any divinely ordered circumstances with which they may be historically interwoven, the result contemplated in the purpose of God is realized in a progressive revelation of his wisdom, righteousness, and grace for the instruction and moral elevation of men. The revelation so produced is permanent and infallible for all matters of faith and practice; except so far as any given revelation may be manifestly partial, provisional, and limited in its time and conditions, or may be afterwards modified or superseded by a higher and fuller revelation, adapted to an advanced period in the redemp-

tive process to which all revelation relates as its final end and glorious consummation.

It is on the *a posteriori* principle that we have been working. In the preceding chapters we have attempted a survey of the whole ground, noting the characteristic phenomena of the collection of books called Holy Scripture, referring to the salient points and most remarkable facts, and at last summed them up in what we have now given. There is not a point that had not been provided for in the preceding exhibit.

Yet full as the definition is, it needs supplementing, and the supplement also has been anticipated. It lies very near, and we must have it if we would understand the subject in its breadth, and must use it for our final relief. Confusion might result from an endeavor to include it in the same formula. Its proper place is close alongside, where we can pass easily from one to the other. We shall find our way to it presently.

The above definition in its reference to "progressive revelation" and human development, is intended to provide for disclosures of truth suited to the stage of moral and spiritual growth that had been reached when it was made. The inspiring energy did not confer omniscience, and did not lift its subjects so far above the plane of thought that characterized their age as to be out of touch with it.

Our conception admits that together with the clearer apprehension and higher moral tone that resulted from the supernatural quickening of his faculties, enabling the prophet at times to discover truth before unrevealed, a commingling of human misconception was suffered to remain till the time should come for further disclosure. The revelation that could at first be apprehended by human capacity was of a very low grade. As imperfectly appropriated, it might give rise to deeds of loyalty to the divine will, expressing savage detestation of heathenism, that seem shocking to us, and impossible to reconcile with the highest moral excellence. This is the revelation which the definition refers to as "partial, provisional, and limited to its own time." Of the test by which this may be determined we shall speak presently.

It is often asserted most positively in controversy with those who refer discriminatively to different parts of the Bible, assigning a higher value to the later than to the earlier revelation, that the Old Testament, as well as the New, is perfect and infallible in its minutest details. The highest inspiration is claimed equally for every part. But who can say intelligently, in this sweeping sense, that the entire Bible, for all time is "the perfect and infallible rule of faith and practice," or any one Book in the Old Testament? To press this familiar statement from the Confession against those who find serious imperfections in the earlier Scriptures, is mere jugglery of words. No one who uses it against others as condemnatory, believes it himself of the Old Testament apart from the New. If we would avoid confusion of thought, nothing is more important than reasonable discrimination.

XX.

THE DEFINITION COMPLETED AND THE FINAL TEST.

We shall not have fulfilled our proposed task until we have reached a satisfactory conclusion for disturbed minds with regard to the varying degrees of certainty in the Bible which the foregoing definition assumes. This may mean, in the estimation of many, uncertainty everywhere, interminable perplexity whenever they open the Bible.

They may feel obliged to accept our conclusions, as apparently founded on a correct view of its character and contents. Nevertheless they are distressed, and almost wish they had been left in their previous contentment. They had supposed it was all holy ground, and they might plant their foot firmly in all its borders. But now they shall fear quagmires and quicksands at every step. The thought of this is almost enough to engulf them in John Bunyan's allegorical *Slough of Despond*. Even a "Thus-saith-the-Lord" seems to be no guarantee against principally human derivation, and a consequent impairment of the divine thought. This is even worse than impairment by copyists or translators. "Where are we," they ask, "and where, if anywhere, shall we find safety?"

THE DEFINITION COMPLETED. 167

We should not have commenced this work, if we could not, anticipating such questions, have furnished a reply that shall more than renew their former confidence. While we have appeared to be doing harm, we shall have done immeasurable good.

Is there anything in the Bible,—it seems a strange question, but we must ask it,—that is not inspired? We do not refer to language attributed to Satan or to evil-minded men. There is plenty of that. But look in the opposite direction. Are there statements or communications *superior* to anything to be thought of as inspired? If we hesitate, he that now speaketh to us from heaven himself shall give answer, and his words are faithful and true: "*Whosoever drinketh of the water that I shall give him shall never thirst; but the water that I shall give him shall become in him a well of water springing up unto eternal life.*"

Is it asked again, "How shall I find my way to the fountain of truth, that drinking I may live forever?" Again the answer—this also is in the first person singular, and is decisive: "*I am the way, and the truth, and the life; no one cometh to the Father but through me.*"

We are now ready for an emphatic statement, supplementary to our definition. It was not long enough.

No proposed definition of God's inspiring grace can be accepted as complete unless it has been formulated (1) *in the light of the grand central truth in which inspiration and revelation alike culminate, that Jesus Christ as a person, " the Only-begotten of the Father," is the final, perfect, and the only perfect revelation of God to men ; and* (2) *with due regard to the radical difference between the words of Christ, who is himself the truth, and those of all inspired teachers, as between the primary and every secondary source of divine knowledge and authority.*

To this must be added a companion sentence that leads us one step further in the attempted reconstruction. Both have been provided for in preceding chapters.

(1) *All historic, prophetic, and didactic revelation of God in the inspired Books of the Old and New Testaments, is inferior and subordinate to his revelation of personal truth and grace in the Christ of the historic Gospels ; and* (2) *whatsoever the former may contain that is incongruous therewith, whatever be the explanation of the incongruity, is not to be held as authoritative for us, but is virtually superseded, as an imperfect and provisional inspiration.*

Shall we put one more question growing out of the uncertainty of merely human sources, even if inspired, and test his ability to answer ? There can be no jugglery here. We have found one who can probe the depths of our hearts, while he reveals to us the heart of God. We may ask confidently :

How may one know beyond doubt that the words of Christ recorded in the Gospels actually contain the living truth he is in search of ?

The ready answer comes, and indeed it is probing : " *He that will do his will shall know the teaching,*

THE DEFINITION COMPLETED. 169

whether it be of God, or whether I have spoken of myself."

It depends, then, upon ourselves, and suggests the heart-searching question, Do I give myself up absolutely to the control of God, sincerely desiring to do his will, if I may only know it? Then shall we know the truth, and shall be prepared to say, "Lord, to whom shall we go? thou hast the words of eternal life, and we believe and know that thou art the Christ, the Son of the living God."

If this surrender is thorough and unreserved, our trouble is ended. No clouds and darkness henceforth —no fog-banks intercepting the divine light—no quicksands and quagmires. We go forward with unfaltering step. We shall walk in the light as God is in the light, shall have fellowship one with another, and the blood of Jesus his Son cleanseth us from all sin. Verily we have found an highway, a royal road, on which the sun always shines. It leads up to "the city whose gates are of pearl, and its streets of pure gold, and which hath no need of the sun, neither of the moon to shine upon it, for the glory of God doth lighten it and the Lamb is the light thereof."

The riddles that have embarrassed us shall all be solved now, or those which we cannot or need not solve, we shall be able to cast aside as frivolous, or will class them with "the secret things that belong unto the Lord our God," and be perfectly content. It is all in his hands, and some things we can take upon trust. Enough for us that in all matters of importance our doubts shall be dissipated forever.

We have been troubled about Old Testament revelation, its alleged uncertainties, inaccuracies, and contradictions, and even about some things more distressing, enormities that make our blood run cold as we read of them. And some earnest souls are kept back from the central truth by the antecedent revelation with its historic and moral perplexities. May we not avoid them, at least for the present, until we can return to them more safely?

The Old Testament is supposed to be the porch to the New, its only proper entrance. This is all very well for those who lived before the coming of Christ. They might find their way to him, at least prospectively, through the previous inspiration. They could do no better.

But we now living did not enter upon our earthly existence under such limitations, and may approach him directly. It is vastly better than coming to him through tortuous passages with uncertain glimmer of light, and sometimes questionable footing. It is our privilege, Jew or Gentile, founded upon our historic position, to go straight to the divine Master's feet, and to ask all the questions we wish. He has ascended on high, but not beyond our call. We need not go a pilgrimage even to Judea in order to find him. For he said while yet here: "*If any man love me, he will keep my words; and my Father will love him, and we will come unto him, and make our abode with him.*" And perhaps he has left with us answers to our questions that will give us rest.

A year or two ago we came upon a remarkable

book: "The great discourse of Jesus, the Christ, the Son of God. A topical arrangement and analysis of all his words, recorded in the New Testament, separated from the Context."* The compiler, a layman eminent in culture and position, has suppressed his own name. This may have been desired thus to give himself more freedom in relating his personal experience in a prefacing *Apologia*.

His work is well done. His classification of the material of our Saviour's discourses is intelligent and faithful. It will convince many that the teachings of our Lord are much more comprehensive than they had supposed, and of greater value than all prophetic and apostolic inspiration combined.

In the above mentioned *Apologia* he speaks of the work as the outcome of his own search after spirit and life, the results of which were so satisfactory as to induce the hope that it might be of use beyond his own personal need. We introduce this individual experience in illustration of the possibility that every disturbed soul may attain peace and rest by the method we have already indicated.

He describes his early condition in the following sentences: " At middle life I found myself without a creed,—a Christian neither in faith or work, out of sympathy with Christian ethics as adapted to the use of modern society, and deeply antagonistic to organic Christianity as manifested in the Church. . . . . I was drifting rapidly away from the religious traditions of my youth, flying no flag, yet not prepared to cast overboard the banner of the Cross, my course dark-

* A. D. F. Randolph & Co., New York, 1892.

ened by speculative doubts, and the philosophic craft, such as it was, in which I had embarked my soul battered by continual and bitter tempests."

But at last he summoned courage to escape from the conflict and suffering: "There came a time, however, that I felt that I must get my bearings and know plainly where I lay with reference to the God of my youth,—his dealings with me and mine with him,—or that I must face, godless and alone, that gray, awful waste of waters whose horizon is eternity, with no polestar in the infinite night, and no hope of a haven at any time. To live longer in such a state was neither honest nor tolerable. Far better to utterly renounce,—if so be I must, even though the renunciation stripped bare,—than cling against conviction to a sentiment, however consoling, enshrined in a fable, however beautiful, for fear of the desolation that would follow its loss."

Of two things he presently became convinced: the first, that he knew very little of the bearing and import of Christ's teaching; the second, that his mental attitude towards Christ had relation almost entirely to the historical and physical phenomena of his life, and not to the divine element which it manifested. And further that in rationalistic assaults upon Christianity the line of attack was necessarily over the same field. "The assault was ever upon the man-Christ, upon the supposition that that once destroyed, the God-Christ of necessity disappeared; whereas it now began to occur to me that the God-Christ loomed infinitely out of range, and could be

THE DEFINITION COMPLETED. 173

reached by no bullet of logic, or of empirical synthesis, and that once apprehended, the man-Christ became invulnerable." .... "I therefore made up my mind to acquaint myself with Christ's doctrine in his own words, apart from any consideration of the narrative context, taking it <u>directly from the</u> <u>lips</u> of the Master, and meditating upon it in the quiet of my own soul, free from the noise of controversy, theological or rational. .... To us who have not lived in the wondrous aura of the spiritual life that radiated from his wondrous personality, who cannot drink from his lips, nor look into the infinite depths of his eyes, the closest touch must lie in the words that were spoken for us, and for all time to come,—the body in which he still lives for us, and which he knew must satisfy our hunger and thirst for truth."

And so, finding truth and life in Christ, he came forth from perplexity and peril into the light of God.

XXI.

THE FINAL TEST—CONTINUED.

In ocean travel a vessel is liable to be driven aside by counter currents and adverse winds the effects of which the mariner may not observe till he finds himself on a lee shore, with the roar of the breakers in his ears, and sail power and steam are alike unavailing. It is said that an air-ship, rising above the lower atmosphere in which it would be driven wildly along, the sport of fierce and threatening blasts, will ascend into a serene stratum above the clouds, where the sun is always shining, and steady, gentle breezes are ever bearing in one invariable direction, and those who shape the course may lay it toward the point that shall best accomplish the object of the voyage and bring them to their haven in safety. It may be an unproved theory, but it will serve for illustration.

The suggestion in our quotations in the last chapter is similar,—that in order to reach the ultimate, satisfying truth,—that is, to reach God,—we may avoid embarrassment, conflict, and the danger of final disappointment and despair, by going directly to the heart of Christ, which is the heart of God, for He said, "*I and the Father are one.*"

For the time being we look only Christ-ward, and

THE FINAL TEST. 175

find relief from the perplexity produced by the crudities and obscurities of a preparatory and provisional inspiration,—one that took men in ignorance, sensuality, and barbarism, and did for them what it could at the time. We leave all that behind. No distortions, exaggerations, or suggestions of improbability, materialistic or metaphysical, confront us here. We are upon higher ground, where those who deal in such objections to revealed truth are too shrewd to interfere with us. With regard to the truths we meet here, with affectation of superior wisdom they call themselves agnostics. They have to decline any direct and positive opposition. It is an atmosphere they cannot breathe. They hear a language they do not understand, which appeals to faculties they consciously do not possess. So with vision undiverted and undisturbed we behold the truth and the life issuing from the lips and throbbing in the pulses of the Son of God. We drink in the words of which he who uttered them said, "*They are spirit, and they are life.*"

Where is Moses, and where are the Levite and the priest? Where is David with his songs, and where are Isaiah and Ezekiel with their glowing visions? Where even are Paul and John? They spake concerning the truth, as "they were moved by the Holy Ghost," and are to be honored as living oracles of God. But he is the truth, the truth incarnate, personal. They receive witness of men, that their writings are not fiction, and the evidence adduced may be met by plausible contradiction. We may not receive their words till they are satisfactorily attested. But he needs no witness of men, and his words sink into hearts by their own intrinsic weight. "*He that believeth hath the witness in himself.*" "*I am the light of the world. He that believeth in me shall not walk in darkness, but shall have the light of life.*" What prophet or apostle could say that,—feeble taper that he is even at his brightest shining?

But what proof have we that the words recorded ever passed from his lips? Why, from what source could they have proceeded, save his unique personality, in which the most exquisite human sympathy is blended with divine knowledge, compassion, and power? Who but he who "knew what was in man" could so strike the chords that thrill all human hearts with the deepest, purest, and most controlling emotions? Human reason and invention stand bewildered before the majesty, sweetness, and power of his sentences,—cannot sound their unfathomable depths,—can only talk in a confused way of the historic antecedents or accompaniments in the same volume, as being here and there improbable, contradictory, or perhaps morally objectionable.

What care we? His words are the cream and essence—the quintessence and soul of all truth,—food for immortal spirits. They exalt, they strengthen, they enlarge, they purify, they inspire confidence and hope, they scatter the mists, and peace such as the world cannot give—the peace that passeth all understanding—takes permanent possession of our hearts.

The historical investiture may have suffered somewhat through the imperfection of human instruments of record. Material information that might have removed all difficulty may have been omitted. Many of us are ignorant and helpless in argument against trained and skillful objectors,—as helpless as the blind man in the hands of Pharisaic tormentors who could only say, "One thing I know, that whereas I was blind, now I see." What other thing did he need to know, or what did he care for, in comparison with this,—he that now for the first time beheld the light of the sun,—and who could convince him that he was laboring under a delusion?

But can we rely, some one may persist in asking, upon these words in the Gospel as really his own? He will himself answer: "But the Comforter, which is the Holy Spirit, whom the Father will send unto you, he shall teach you all things, and bring all things to your remembrance, whatsoever I have said unto you." And then we try them intrinsically, as he invited us, and we find them a specific, a panacea. There are healing, soundness, and life in them, and we dwell in peace. Objections on lower ground are idle and wasted breath. The ground of our conviction they do not even touch. We might afford, although we will not, to give up miracles, to give up inspiration, to give up historic confirmation, as men give odds at games of strength and skill, and should abide in confidence and win the day. "Evidence of Christianity," said a man of deep thought, "evidence of Christianity; make a man feel the want of it, rouse him to the self-knowledge of his need of it, and you may safely trust it to its own evidence."

We have made above, somewhat separately, two points that are of the first importance and ever to be remembered. The *first* is, that he who came from heaven to identify himself with men gave his personal assurance that his words should be correctly reported. Through his Holy Spirit, the revealer of truth, he would look after this matter himself. The *second* is, that he ascribed to his own words a special potency, a spirit and life, by which they should be distinguished to the inmost consciousness of him who receives them in humble faith, from all others. They should be a revelation of the Son of God within him.* Their spirit and life should become elements in his being, enabling him to say, "It is no longer I that live, but Christ liveth in me; and the life which I now live in the flesh, I live by faith, the faith which is of the Son of God, who loved me, and gave himself for me." †

We reverse, then, the usual order of suggestion, for those who are painfully anxious to know whether in this Bible we have the saving word of God. We do not ask a man to satisfy himself by careful study with innumerable preliminaries in an older revelation, some of which are adapted to times and circumstances into which we cannot transport ourselves, the nature and needs of which we cannot comprehend, and which have suffered we know not how

---

* Gal. i. 16. † Gal. ii. 20.

much from the ravages of time, and the ignorance or presumption of men, sometimes pious and well-meaning. What care we for such a revelation, although otherwise of immense interest and value, in comparison with "the light of the knowledge of the glory of God in the face of Jesus Christ" as we now gaze upon it? We have found him of whom Moses and the prophets wrote, we hear his words, and in them we discover the heart of God as our Almighty Father and everlasting Friend. We know the truth, and it has made us free indeed, and free forever.

In this conviction we are ready now for the Old Testament. We may be reasonably asked by any inquirer after truth, If the Bible was given by inspiration of the Spirit, and contains great thoughts of God, of imperishable value, and yet is full of imperfections, how shall I discriminate between the better and the worse? If, besides the divine truth that it embodies, it also contains partial truths, which are sometimes as misleading as falsehood, and moral incongruities and monstrosities from which our souls recoil, how shall I separate the gold from the dross? By the use of my reason? Would you have me become a rationalist?

Yes, rather than be a sophist or a simpleton. Yes, a thousand times, if one becomes a rationalist by making use of his reason, including conscience and every spiritual faculty with which God has endowed him, strengthened and enlightened by the word, and life, and spirit of Christ. Who will fling a gibe at us for such rationalism—a rationalism that verges so closely upon inspiration?

This is the final and decisive test of all utterances or writings known among men. Having the principal, central, all-embracing truth embedded in our hearts, "we have an unction from the Holy One and know all things." We go fearlessly, therefore, to the old inspiration, approving or rejecting, as it may be. If anything agrees not with these words of Christ in the Gospels, and with the life of God incarnate, as illustrating his words,—no matter how it came to be what it is, no matter to whose ignorance and hardness of heart it may have been adaptively lowered,—polygamy, slavery, revenge, and barbarity of every kind,—we renounce and denounce it as evil. Our enlightened moral instinct rejects it unreservedly and forever. Any disciple of Christ that does not speak according to this word knows not what spirit he is of. Let him come closer to Christ in his pervasive, effluent, and communicative moral purity. Let him take John's position, pillowing his head on the Master's bosom, where he can hear his faintest whisper and feel every throb of his pure, tender, and loving heart, and he will come to a better mind.

Yes, this is the final and decisive test, from which there can be no appeal to a higher court, and we offer it as a relief from all difficulty, as respects the principal point we have considered. We reaffirm unfalteringly our proposition, as the most incontestable of moral axioms, that *whatsoever in the Old Testament revelation, or in any professed revelation from God, is not in accord with the revelation of his righteousness, or purity, or love, or truth, in the words and life of Christ, has been annulled and superseded, and is practically no revelation for us.*

There can be no modification of this sweeping judgment. It must stand for all time, challenging disproof or contradiction. Yet any reasonable relief that may be possible shall be cheerfully accorded. We must not be misunderstood for a moment. And therefore an emphatic restatement of earlier thought may be suffered together with some additions.

It is not the mutilation of the Bible that we suggest, as if all enormities should be stricken from the record of fact. Even for us they have their moral uses, if only by repulsion, as we contrast them with the higher law and the purer morality under which we are living.

They have also severally their historic accompaniment, which relieves some of their worst features. If we sit in judgment, in any given instances upon record, upon the *men*, whose thoughts and practices were so far below the standard that has been prescribed for our own regulation that we instinctively reprobate them, our judgment must be mitigated by important extenuating circumstances, which are righteously considered in every court of justice before sentence is pronounced. These circumstances may impart a different aspect both to their own conduct and to the divine rule under which was permitted the moral evil that shocks us. Every special transaction that comes under review is part of an extended narrative. It has its background, and its foreground, —a lower morality in the past, and a higher in the future.

This semi-barbarous people had their moral law. Whatever may have been its imperfections, it was gradually but surely regenerative. It was educating their conscience, although on account of their depressed moral status in a very rude way. They were in a low form in the school of their divine Teacher, but they were in, and not outside of, his school. They were being taught that men were so far above the brutes that they could recognize a personal God. They enjoyed the dignity of being persons. They were also learning that they were morally responsible,—that there were some things that they might not do without incurring the displeasure of their Lawgiver.

And further, if a command issued by a divinely appointed leader is intolerably repulsive to us, it was not so to *them*. We who have attained higher forms in the world-wide schoolroom of the great Instructor of men, may find occasion in these narratives to bless him for the results of his wise, pure, and faithful teaching, in the moral sensibilities that stir our hearts when we read what horrid things were done by those of our own race only a few centuries ago, without a thought of their being evil.

The men whose lives we are contemplating with aversion were on the ascending grade. They were in the firm grasp of one who was bearing the race they represented forward and upward. The results of his teaching will appear further on, and its wisdom and effectiveness will be fully justified.

Take for example the butcheries in Canaan under Joshua. A little while before their historic time, those who committed them, like those they exterminated as wild beasts, would have performed such cruelties for cruelty's sake. But now, conscience was being exercised. This was quite a new thing in the earth. There could have been no such lessons inculcated in the school of Moloch, Baal, or Astarte. As reasons for the act, they were told of the gross corruptions to which these people were addicted. The subsequent extermination was not the wanton and unmitigated barbarity it must otherwise have been. They were taught practically to detest as horrible and hateful the forms of wickedness that were branded as evil in their own law.

It is true that lessons of the sacredness of human life, and of tenderness, pity, and brotherly-kindness with which we are so familiar, were strikingly absent here. But these were among the advanced lessons of the future, which should at last purge the earth from all its wickedness. Give them time. From the nature of the case everything cannot be done at once for men in the moral degradation and imperviousness to right impressions from which they were gradually being rescued.

We thus see what deep and far-reaching principles lie here. Do not mutilate the Book, nor expunge even a single page. It may not be very pleasant reading—quite the opposite. But if we study it carefully, the foulest record has its indirect moral uses for all the world. It would be a miserably superficial thought,—no one in his right senses would entertain it,—that because such things were done several thousand years ago under apparent divine sanction, they were morally right. We are not to call evil *good*, nor good *evil*, because something on the surface of the Bible in early times of moral stupidity seems to obliterate moral distinctions.

There might be in the divine rule some temporary accommodation to hardness of heart, in view of the fact that softening influences were at work. But bad is bad, all the world over and for all time, and it never can be good. We must not suffer the moral sensitiveness that is the greatest glory of our nature, and which under the teaching of Christ is becoming exquisitely true and sound in its judgments, to become blunted by such records of far-off facts and ethical conditions different from our own.

Let it be conceded that a long time ago God mercifully "overlooked" some things that are unspeakably evil. Yet he now commands all men everywhere to repent of and abjure them. Thank God that we have become so sensitive to such evil that we shrink from it with wondering horror through the teaching and example of our blessed Saviour and the grace of his transforming Spirit.

We take, then, an enlightened view of the divine government under the mysteries that formerly enwrapped it. We can look with some leniency at these men of old,—savage, yet human like ourselves.

THE FINAL TEST. 185

Such might we have been but for God's grace. But when we have regard to the *evil itself*, apart from these extenuating considerations, we condemn it unsparingly as its moral enormity deserves. The ruling that permitted it still stands, as part of the record of irreversible facts. But we now judge of this ruling by a later and more perfect divine revelation. As respects the regulation of our own lives, the former is abolished and superseded. The holy light in which we live reveals the true character of the deeds here described, and for our thought and practice such Scripture has no authority. Moral offences so unspeakably evil, we repel and detest under the higher law and illumination of Christ. That they are in the Bible need not trouble us in the least.

We repeat then with emphasis our axiom, and without abatement: *Whatsoever in the Old Testament revelation, or in any professed revelation from God, is not in accord with the righteousness, or love, or purity, or truth, in the words and the life of Christ, has been annulled and superseded, and is practically no revelation for us.*

The errancy of Scripture disturbs us no more. Christ himself is our pattern and law, which can never fail us. The all-perfect revelation of the glory of God in the person, life, and instructions of our divine Redeemer, is like the electric search-light so important in our modern naval warfare. It dissipates all darkness, and exposes to detestation everything contrary to God and his law in thought, or word, or deed.

It sweeps over the vast spaces that separate us from man's first existence upon the earth. No subtle illusions, no ingenious sophistries, no artful disguises that error or wickedness may assume, no fog-banks of falsehood and wrong can withstand its penetrative gleam.

This light of light illumines all history. Before it centuries and eons are like moments and hours. It tests all that the busy brain of man has conceived, his hands have wrought or his fingers have recorded in whatever character or on whatever material, whether on parchment or on clay, on brass or on stone. It is "living and powerful, and sharper than any two-edged sword, and piercing to the dividing asunder of soul and spirit, of both the joints and the marrow, and quick to discern the thoughts and intents of the heart."

Nothing that claims to be sacred may decline its scrutiny, for nothing can be more sacred than itself. No prophet, no apostle, no Moses, David, or Isaiah of the Old Testament, or Paul or John of the New, would shrink back or cower before this holy light; " for every one that doeth the truth cometh to the light, that his deeds may be made manifest that they are wrought in God." Even in the writings of these it separates the purely human from the divine; and in whatever is produced conjointly, it separates the temporary, partial, and provisional, as accommodated to immaturity and incapacity, from that which must abide in unchanging glory like the years of the Most High.

Then in all darkness, and in all doubt and perplexity, as between truth and error, the right and the wrong, the work of God and the work of Apollyon, who hides his missiles of destruction under dark coverts and in deep waters, *bring out the Search-light,* "the true light that lighteth every man, coming into the world." Its hostility to all deeds of darkness is uncompromising and deadly.

But it lovingly recognizes, enfolds, and absorbs, to give forth again with added splendor, whatever it shines upon that is akin to its own substance and nature, which is in fact only an irradiation from itself, though it may have been glowing in brightness for ten thousand years. For this is the primeval light, in comparison with which, or apart from which, all other light is darkness.

To the glory of the Lord of light we have performed our work. May he graciously accept it.

www.ingramcontent.com/pod-product-compliance
Lightning Source LLC
Chambersburg PA
CBHW021734220426
43662CB00008B/850